3.99

Your Baby's First Year
MONTH *by* MONTH

Your Baby's First Year

MONTH *by* MONTH

ALISON MACKONOCHIE

STRATHEARN BOOKS LIMITED
Toronto, Canada

A VERY SPECIAL THANK YOU TO ROBIN FOR HIS UNFAILING SUPPORT, TO LUCY AND KATE, WITHOUT WHOM WE WOULD NOT HAVE HAD CHRISTMAS, AND TO DOMINIC FOR JUST BEING HIMSELF.

First published in 1996 by Ultimate Editions

Ultimate Editions is an imprint of
Anness Publishing Limited
Boundary Row Studios
1 Boundary Row
London SE1 8HP

This edition published by
STRATHEARN BOOKS LIMITED
Toronto, Canada

Previously published as part of a larger compendium, *The Complete Book of Pregnancy & Babycare*.

A CIP catalogue record for this book is available from the British Library.

ISBN 1-86035-054-2

Publisher: Joanna Lorenz
Project Editors: Casey Horton, Nicky Thompson
Editor: Elizabeth Longley
Designer: Bobbie Colgate Stone
Jacket Designer: Patrick Mcleavey & Partners
Special Photography: Alistair Hughes
Additional Photography: Carin Simon
Illustrations: Ian Sidaway
Hair and Make-up: Bettina Graham

Printed in Singapore by Star Standard Industries Pte. Ltd.

2 4 6 8 10 9 7 5 3 1

CONTENTS

INTRODUCTION

YOUR NEWBORN arrives in the world a helpless, totally dependent baby, yet, with your help, within a year she will have learned all the basic skills that she needs to build on for her future growth and development. This book takes you, month by month, through the first year of a child's development. It is, however, important to realize that your child is unique, so there is little point in comparing her with others in anything other than a general way at this stage.

You will want to help and encourage your child as she masters each new skill. Understanding how she learns to talk, crawl, walk and play will enable to you to assist her at each stage. The five senses - hearing, vision, taste, smell and touch - are all extremely important from the time your child is born. As each sense develops, your child will be discovering something new about the world in which she's living.

Being able to participate in this fascinating time in your child's life is a very special privilege. You will be part of the most exciting process in the world: the development of your child from a helpless baby to a confident, independent toddler.

NEWBORN

Your newborn baby will probably look wrinkled and slightly blotchy at first. When he is born his skin may have a bluish tinge and the legs may even be a different colour to the rest of his body. This will only last for a short time, until oxygen from the lungs has had time to reach the bloodstream. You may also find patches of dry skin. Eyes may be reddish and slightly swollen and your baby may still be covered with vernix, the greasy white substance which has been protecting the skin from becoming waterlogged by the amniotic fluid. There may also be a covering of lanugo, fine hair which covers the shoulders, upper arms, and legs.

Your baby's head may look too big for his body. It is usually about one-quarter of the total body length and it may be a slightly odd shape because of the pressure that was put on it during the birth. His features may also appear slightly flattened from being squeezed through the pelvis. Your baby's head may be covered with very thin hair or have a thick thatch that stands up on end.

Milestones

Your child is immediately able to:
• Hear and respond to noises.
• Focus on objects that are within 20-30 cm/8-12 in.
• Grip your finger tightly.
• Suck vigorously.
• Make walking movements when held on a hard surface.
• Turn towards you when you stroke his cheek.

An increase in female hormones from the placenta just before birth affects both boys and girls and your baby's genitals may be enlarged and breasts may appear slightly swollen.

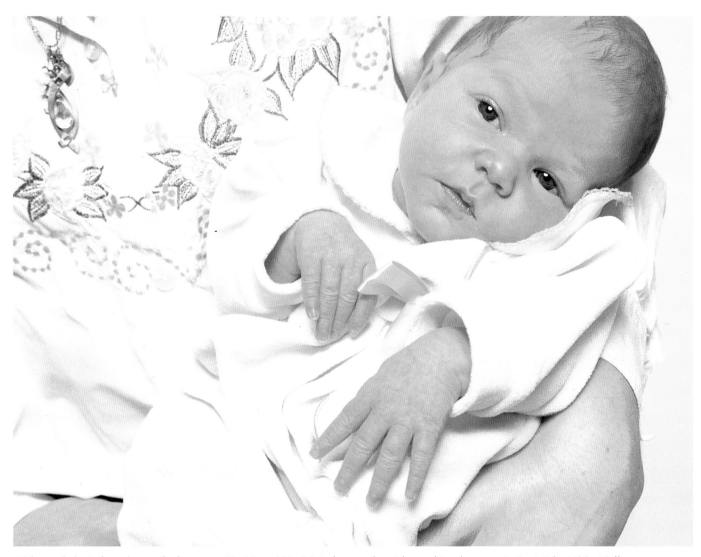

When a baby is born he can be between 45–55 cm/18–22 in long and weigh anything between 2.5–4.5 kg/5½–10 lb.

It is quite usual for the breasts of both boys and girls to have a milky discharge; girls may have a slight vaginal discharge as well. All these features will disappear over the next few weeks.

SIZE

Although the average weight of a baby at birth is 3.4 kg/7½ lb, wide variations occur so, assuming that your baby was born around the estimated date of delivery (EDD), it could weigh anything between 2.5-4.5 kg/5½-10 lb. Your baby's weight is determined by a lot of factors, including your size and the size of your partner, how much weight you put on in pregnancy, and your general health.

Your baby is quite likely to lose weight during the first week. This is because it takes a little while for regular feeding to become properly established. Once an infant is feeding well his weight should remain stable for a couple of days and then, within seven to 10 days, he will regain his birth weight. A baby's weight gain is one of the easiest ways of telling whether he is thriving.

The average length of a newborn is between 48-51 cm/19-20 in, but as with weight, this can vary, although most babies are somewhere between 45-55 cm/18-22 in.

REFLEXES

A baby is born with a number of reflexes. The rooting reflex means that your child's mouth automatically searches for your nipple; grasping is seen when your baby demonstrates a surprisingly strong grip. When on his back, your baby may adopt the tonic neck reflex – the head is turned to one side and the arm and leg on that side are extended while the opposite ones are flexed. A loud noise or the sensation of falling causes the startle or Moro reflex: the newborn extends legs, arms, and fingers, arches the back and throws the head back and then draws back the arms, fists clenched, into the chest. All these initial reflexes will gradually diminish over the next weeks and months as voluntary movements take their place.

In addition to these reflexes, every baby is born with the ability to suck, swallow, and gag so that they can feed as soon as they are born. The gagging reflex prevents a baby from choking on too much liquid and allows the child to get rid of any mucus that may be blocking up his airways.

Your newborn will probably hiccup and snuffle a lot at first. Hiccups occur because the baby's breathing rhythm is still rather jerky. They

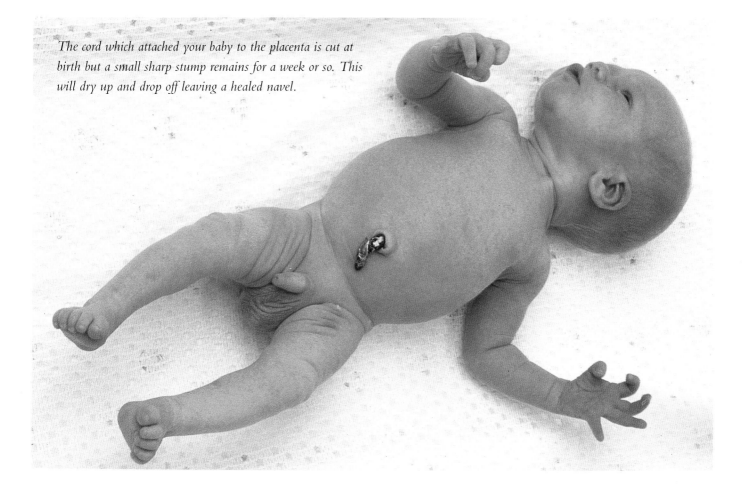

The cord which attached your baby to the placenta is cut at birth but a small sharp stump remains for a week or so. This will dry up and drop off leaving a healed navel.

don't hurt, or even particularly bother them in fact, so you need not worry about them at all. Your baby will also make some snuffling noises. This is from learning to breathe through his nose and because the nasal passages are still very small. As the nose gets bigger the snuffling will stop.

All babies are sensitive to bright lights and this may make them sneeze when they first open their eyes. This is because the light stimulates the nerves in their nose as well as their eyes. Sneezing is also a way of clearing the nasal passages and it will prevent any dust from getting into the baby's lungs.

CRYING

Your baby may make his first cry as soon as his chest has been delivered, others wait until they have been born or until they start to breathe normally. These first cries are often not much more than a whimper and the full-bodied cry follows later. A baby may look red and angry while crying, but this is quite normal. Crying is a baby's way of communicating as well as a means of exercising his lungs.

Hunger is the main reason for a newborn to cry, but being lonely, wet, or tired will also make a baby cry. Some babies cry because they don't like being undressed, others

when they are immersed in water. Some babies are more fretful than others so they cry more. You will quickly learn to recognize why your baby is crying and the best way to soothe him.

NEWBORN TESTS

The first test your baby will be given is the Apgar test. The scores are recorded at one minute after birth and then again at five minutes and they reflect your newborn's general condition. Babies who score between 7 and 10 are in good to excellent condition, those who score between 4 and 6 are in fair condition, but may need some resuscitative

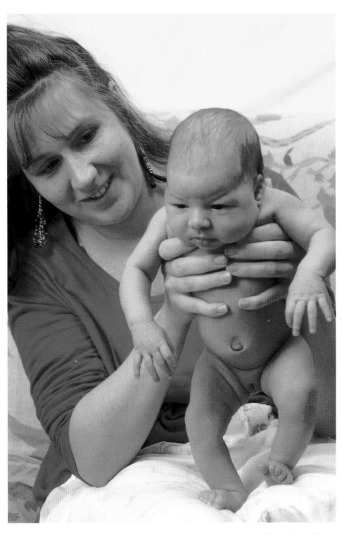

A newborn baby might initially have a stepping reflex, but this will soon be replaced by voluntary movements.

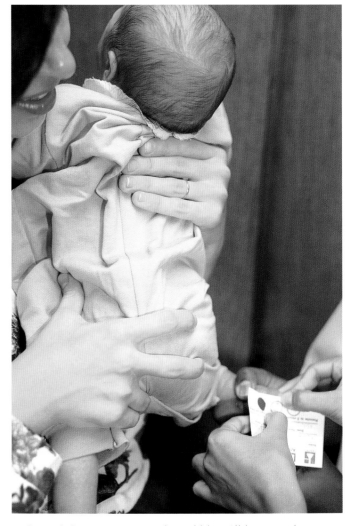

When a baby is six or seven days old he will be given the Guthrie test to test for a range of rare diseases.

Apgar table

Score	0	1	2
Appearance (colour)	pale or white	body pink, extremities blue	pink
Heart rate	not detectable	below 100	over 100
Grimace (reflex irritability)	no response to stimulation	grimace	cough, sneeze
Muscle tone	flaccid (no or weak activity)	some movement of extremities	moving
Respiration (breathing)	none	weak, gasping, irregular	crying, regular

measures. Babies who score under 4 will need some immediate emergency treatment.

Sometime during the first 24-48 hours your baby will be thoroughly checked. A doctor will check your baby's head circumference, the fontanelles, and the roof of the mouth to see if there are any abnormalities. The doctor will listen to the heart and lungs and feel your baby's abdomen to check that the internal organs such as kidney, liver, and spleen, are the right shape and size. The genitals are also checked for abnormalities and, if your baby is a boy, the doctor will look to see that both testicles have descended. Hips will be checked for possible dislocation and all the limbs will be inspected to see that they are the right length and are moving correctly. The doctor will run his thumb down the baby's spine to make sure that the vertebrae are in place. The baby's reflexes will also be checked.

The Guthrie test is usually done six or seven days after birth. A blood sample will be taken from the baby's heel. The blood is then tested for phenylketonuria (PKU), a rare disease which causes severe mental handicap, and other rare diseases.

SPECIAL CARE

If your baby is born several weeks early, the birth weight is low, or your child needs extra care for any other reason, he may be put in the Special Care Baby Unit (SCBU). Here the infant will be monitored so that he gets all the special treatment required. It can be distressing to see your baby in a special care unit, especially if he is surrounded by an array of strange equipment. Ask the staff to explain what the equipment is for and why your baby needs it. Try to spend as much time as you can with your baby in special care because, even if you can't pick him up and hold him, your baby will be able to hear your voice and it will soothe him. You will probably be able to touch your baby through the side of the incubator.

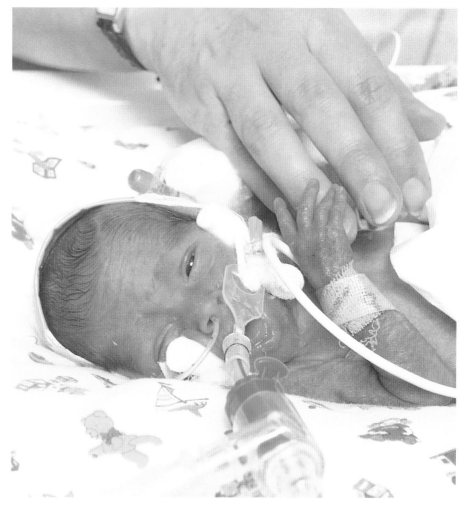

If your baby is born early, he may have to go into the Special Care Baby Unit. Don't be afraid to ask about all the equipment he is attached to, and let him know you are there by touching and talking to him.

ONE MONTH

Your baby's movements are still dominated by the primary reflexes so when placed on her back your infant will adopt the tonic neck reflex posture, with her head to one side and the limbs on that side extended while the ones on the other side are flexed. If you place your baby on her front her head will turn to one side, then your baby will pull her knees under the abdomen and hold her arms close to her body, with her hands curled into fists. The fingers and toes will fan out when she straightens her arms or legs. If you hold your baby to stand on a hard surface she will press down and make a forward walking movement.

Although your baby was born with vision and can see colours and shapes at close range, her sight is still immature. Images which offer a high contrast and simple patterns, for example black lines on a white background, are easier for a baby to understand than paler, more complicated designs. Hold your baby upright or in a half reclining position

Milestones

Your child may be able to:
- Lift her head briefly while lying on her stomach.
- Focus on your face while feeding.
- Respond to a small bell being rung by moving her eyes and head towards the source of the sound.
- Follow with her eyes an object which is moved in an arc 15–25.5 cm/6–10 in away from her face.
- Turn her head towards you when you speak to her.

Even at this early age your baby will be interested in things around him.

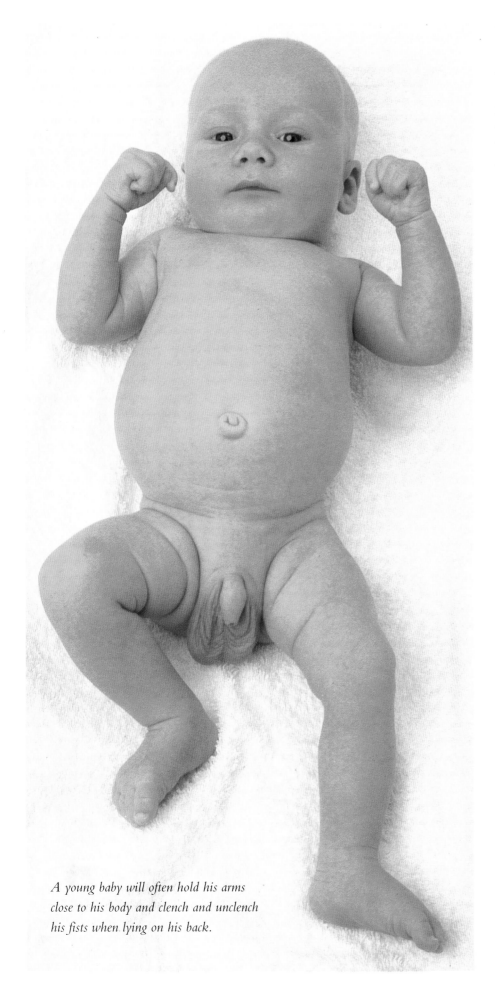

A young baby will often hold his arms close to his body and clench and unclench his fists when lying on his back.

if you are showing her something; this will help to keep the child's interest and will stop her dropping off to sleep. Cot books, with bold patterns and shapes which attract very young eyes, placed where a baby can see them will help develop visual powers.

Babies can recognize their mother's smell from the earliest days and your baby will be able to distinguish between the smell of your breast milk and that of any other mother. She can also tell the difference between the smell of formula or cows' milk and your milk.

MINOR BLEMISHES

Occasionally babies may be born with some minor skin blemishes. These are usually harmless and require no treatment; they disappear on their own as the skin matures. *Milia* are tiny white spots on the face, caused by blocked oil glands. They should fade after a few days. *Stork marks or bites* are red marks which occur around the back of the neck, on the eyelids, or across the bridge of the nose. They usually disappear during the first few months. *Strawberry marks* are raised red marks that sometimes appear in the days after the birth and they may grow rapidly during the first few weeks. These usually disappear after about six months, although they can sometimes last until the child is much older. Treatment may be required if the mark has not disappeared by the time your child is in her teens. *Port wine stains* are red or purple marks which are usually found on the face and neck. These are permanent and will require treatment once your child is older. *Urticaria, or nettle rash* has a raised white centre surrounded by an

A baby needs fresh air so if you have a garden or secure outside area and the weather is warm enough you can let your infant sleep outside in the pram from the first week or so providing that the child is well covered up and away from draughts. When it is hot, use a canopy rather than the pram hood so that the air can circulate, and make sure that the pram is in the shade. When outside, protect your baby from cats and insects with

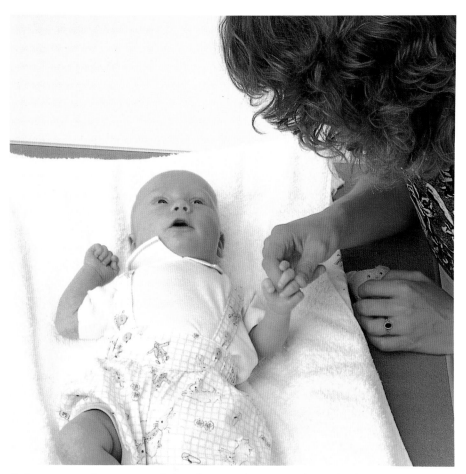

When you are changing your baby, always make time to play and talk to him. This will make him feel secure and at ease.

inflamed red area and quite commonly occurs during the first weeks. This rash doesn't require any treatment and will usually clear up after the first month.

INFECTION

Thrush is a fungal infection that produces white patches on the baby's tongue, the roof of her mouth, and in her cheeks. It can be caught from unsterilized feeding teats and dummies or from the mother if she was suffering from vaginal thrush at the time of the birth. Thrush can also appear on the baby's bottom as a red rash which spreads from the anus over the buttocks. Oral thrush is treated with anti-fungal drops and thrush on a baby's bottom needs to be treated with antibiotic cream. Both can be obtained from your doctor.

Above: White patches on the tongue are one indication that your baby has thrush. This is easily treated.

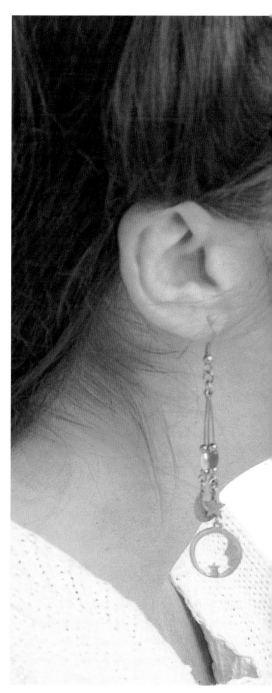

a fine mesh pram net. If you have no place to leave the baby outside, put her in the cot or crib and open the window to let fresh air into the room. Don't leave a baby in her cot or pram for too long when she is awake because she will get bored. Babies need other activities to stimulate them as well as exercise.

Taking your baby on outings in a baby sling or carrier is another way of giving your baby fresh air and a convenient way for you to carry her if you don't want to push a pram. Your baby will enjoy being close to you and will be able to see the world from a different viewpoint.

NOISE

There is no need to tiptoe around or to get people to whisper while your baby is asleep. If you do, it could mean that your baby won't be able to go to sleep if there is any noise and will wake at the least little sound, which can cause sleep problems when your child is older. A very young baby will quickly learn to sleep through the everyday noises that go on in a home, such as the television and vacuum cleaner. Sudden loud noises may wake your baby, but reassurance and a cuddle should soon settle her down again.

When newly born your baby's vision is not well developed, so hold her up to talk to her and let her focus on your face.

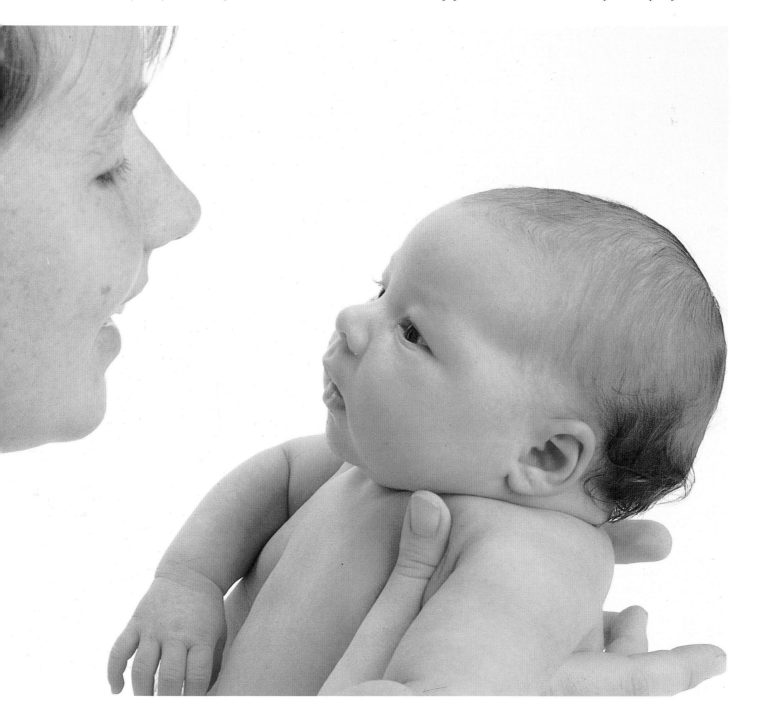

TWO MONTHS

Your baby is developing quickly and, although you may not realize it, he is already trying to talk to you by making a number of vowel sounds and throaty gurgles. At first it may not seem as though these noises are actually directed at you because your baby will enjoy practising these vocal exercises as much for his own benefit as for yours. Each new noise is helping your baby discover which combinations of throat, tongue, and mouth actions make which sounds. As your baby masters each new sound you will begin to notice that he uses them to communicate vocally with you.

CRYING

Your baby now stays awake for longer periods between feeds and is usually more awake in the evenings. It is quite likely that your baby will use some of this extra waking time to cry. Of course not all babies are the same and yours may cry very little, but on average babies usually cry for two to three hours a day and much of this takes place in the evening. Very often this is blamed on colic, thought to be a type of stomach or abdominal ache occurring in spasms, which makes a baby draw up

At two months, your baby will start to smile at you and will turn her head to follow objects moved above her head.

his legs in pain as he screams. No one knows exactly what colic is, but if it is going to occur it usually starts within the first three weeks of birth and lasts until around three months, although it can go on longer. There is no reliable treatment for colic and, although there are some over-the-counter medicines available, you should consult your doctor before giving them to your baby.

Colic isn't always the cause of excessive crying; some babies cry for no obvious reason for some time each day. If your baby does this you may be able to offer comfort by rocking, letting him suck, or by distracting him with a toy. Don't leave

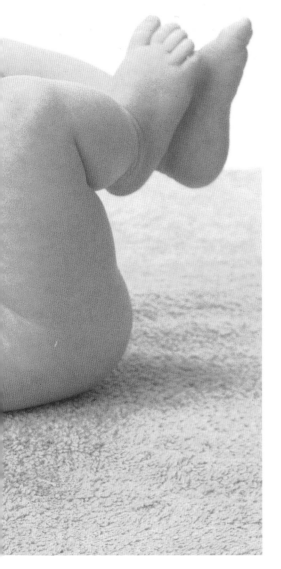

When you support your baby in a sitting position, she can hold her head up for a minute.

Holding and cuddling your young baby is an important part of her getting to know you.

him to cry for more than a few minutes; at this age crying is the only way to let you know that he is miserable and needs comforting.

LEARNING CONTROL

Your baby is gradually gaining control of his body. When you place the child on his stomach he will be able to lift his head, keeping the nose and mouth free to breathe. If held in a sitting position, your baby will be able to hold his head up for about a minute, and if you touch his hand with a rattle your baby will jerk his hand towards it. This is the first stage of learning when he reaches out to hold something.

SIX TO EIGHT WEEK DEVELOPMENT CHECK

The ages at which developmental screening takes place vary within each health authority and with the individual needs of the child. But in general, you can expect your child to have an initial developmental check sometime between six and eight weeks. This will be carried out

Immunization

Your baby should be given the first round of immunizations for diphtheria, tetanus, and whooping cough (DPT), polio and Hib. After the immunization your child may feel a bit off-colour for up to 24 hours and may even run a temperature. Rarely, a convulsion may occur as a result of the fever, but this is over quickly and has no lasting effect. It is also quite normal for the skin around the site of the injection to become red and sore or slightly swollen. If you are at all worried about your child's reaction, contact your doctor immediately.

Learning head movements

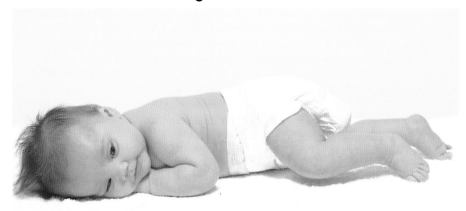

1 *At this stage of development, your baby is gaining control of her body. When lying on her stomach, with her arms supporting her, she can start to lift her head.*

2 *As she manoeuvres herself into position, she pushes hard with her legs and starts to put her weight on her arms.*

3 *As she raises her head, pushing up with her arms, she will find she can hold it up, keeping her nose and mouth free to breathe.*

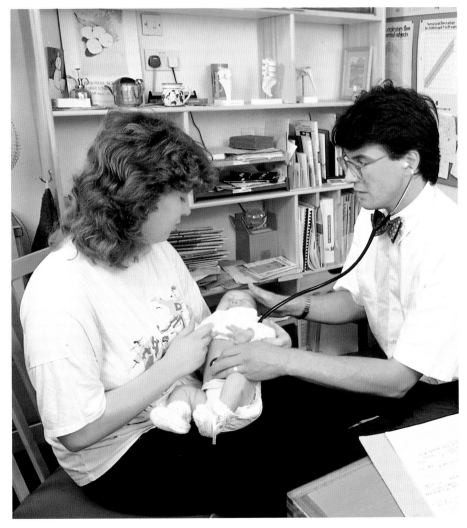

Make sure you allow enough time to play and have fun with your baby, so that you can really get to know her.

at the child health clinic by a doctor or health visitor, or at your doctor's surgery. These checks are part of the child health surveillance programme and their aim is to detect any problems early, to prevent illnesses, and to promote good health. If the checks detect any early signs of delayed development, or health or behaviour problems, treatment can be begun at once. A number of routine checks take place between now and when your child reaches school age. They are all important because the checks are designed to reveal hidden disabilities as well as more obvious ones.

This early check will include measuring your baby's weight, length and head circumference and noting the changes since birth. You will probably be asked questions about how your baby is feeding and sleeping. General progress will be assessed and the doctor may also carry out a series of tests to evaluate your baby's head control, use of hands, vision, hearing, and social interaction. You may be given guidance about what you should expect during the next month in relation to feeding, sleeping, and development. You may also be asked questions about how you, the baby, and the rest of the family are managing with your new baby at home. This is the time to voice any concerns or problems that have been worrying you.

At six to eight weeks your baby will be given a developmental check-up at the health clinic or your doctor's surgery. This will detect any early problems.

THREE MONTHS

Below: As you pull your baby up at this age, he will now be in more control of his head movements.

Your baby will probably have begun to control her head movements, so that when held in a sitting position she can keep her head up for several seconds before it drops forward. As her neck strengthens your baby will be able to look around and turn her head to watch something moving within 15-20 cm/6-8 in.

EARLY LEARNING

As babies begin to understand their own body, they will spend hours studying and moving their fingers. Their hands have opened out now and they can clasp and unclasp them, pressing the palms together. Babies enjoy playing with them and may even be able to hold a small toy for a few seconds. When your baby is lying down you will probably notice that her arms and legs make a lot of

Below: When your baby lies on the floor, he will often raise his head for several seconds before it drops forward.

Below: As your baby sits up, he can hold hishead steady more easily because his neck has strengthened.

Bottom: Your baby will be fascinated by any toys in bright, primary colours that are hung over her cot.

Your child may be able to:

• Smile and coo when she sees you.

• Control her head.

• Show anticipation when food is on the way by licking her lips.

• Enjoy looking at brightly coloured objects such as a mobile hanging over the cot.

• Play with her hands.

• Hold a small toy for a few seconds.

movement. A child will kick vigorously, usually with alternate legs, but occasionally with both legs together.

The first smiles are reflexive, but they very quickly become social and the baby will smile at you in response to your smile or voice. The smiles will come in clusters, four or five at a time, followed by a pause of maybe half a minute before the next cluster. The baby will also respond vocally when you speak to her. Talk

to your baby and she will answer you back in her own way, using her lips and tongue as she coos and tries to imitate you. She uses her whole body to express the way she feels, making excited movements when pleased, expressing happiness and delight with gurgles and squeals. When she is angry, uncomfortable, or lonely she will tell you by crying loudly and even angrily. To encourage your baby, you should respond to her behaviour with exaggerated gestures and praise, using a slow singsong voice and lots of repetition.

A baby will react to familiar situations and will show excitement when she recognizes preparation for things that she enjoys. She responds with obvious pleasure to friendly handling, especially when it is accompanied by play and a friendly voice. Bathtime and other caring routines, where she has your undivided attention for quite a while, are likely to become her favourite times of the day.

Left: Plastic stacking toys in bright colours will soon attract the attention of your inquisitive baby who will try to grasp hold of them.

Below: Lying on his back, your young baby will enjoy kicking vigorously with alternate legs and sometimes with both legs together.

If you haven't already done so, introduce a regular bedtime routine now so that your child starts to realize that a bath, a story, and a cuddle are a prelude to being put into the cot to sleep. By about three months many babies begin to sleep for long periods at night. If your baby has started to sleep through the night you will probably find that she needs less sleep during the day and that her daytime sleep is not as deep as it was. You may find that your baby is more easily disturbed by household noises now. Encourage her to stay awake during the day by stimulating her with different toys and by playing and talking with her.

Immunization

At three months your baby will have the second round of immunizations for diphtheria, tetanus, and whooping cough (DPT), polio and Hib on the immunization programme.

Your baby is now using her whole body to show her feelings, and will start to recognize her favourite toys.

FOUR MONTHS

Your baby is developing rapidly. He is awake for much longer and during these waking periods will want to be sociable and will respond with delight to conversations with you and enjoy playing simple games.

You can encourage your baby's development by spending time responding to these early attempts at sociability. Make a point of showing your baby different objects and talk about them. Your baby will also enjoy seeing and talking to himself in a mirror. Place the mirror about 15-20 cm/6-8 in away so that he can keep his image in focus.

Motor development and learning progress at the same rate between four and five months. Hand and eye co-ordination is being learned and your baby may be able to reach out and grasp an object. He will try hard to learn how to sit because he will have discovered that sitting up gives him a different view of the world. At first he will need you to help him balance, but as his confidence grows he will learn to adjust his legs and to use his hands to keep himself upright.

STARTING ON SOLIDS

Although babies can get all the nourishment they require from breast or formula milk during their first six months, you may want to start to introduce solids at around four months. A baby needs to be able to have control over his head before you begin to offer him solids. Even strained or puréed first foods should not be given until he can hold his head upright when he is sitting propped up. Chunkier foods

At four months your baby will try to sit up with your help.

Milestones

Your child may be able to:

• Lift his head up 90° when he is on his stomach.

• Raise himself up a little way, supported by the arms, when lying on his stomach.

• Laugh out loud.

• Hold his head steady when he is held upright.

• Roll over in one direction.

• Reach out for an object.

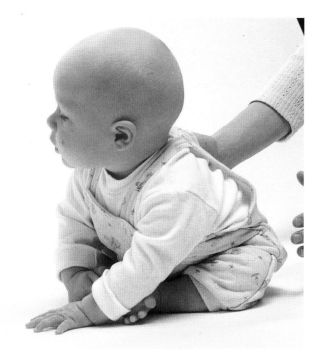

As your baby gains control over his head he will be able to hold it at different angles.

As he gets more active your baby will probably start to learn how to roll over in one direction. First, he will grab his foot with his hand and lift that leg up.

When your baby is lying flat on his stomach, he will now be able to raise his head up 90° and support himself more sturdily on his arms.

He'll then push down this leg, and helped by his bottom arm, roll his body over in one direction.

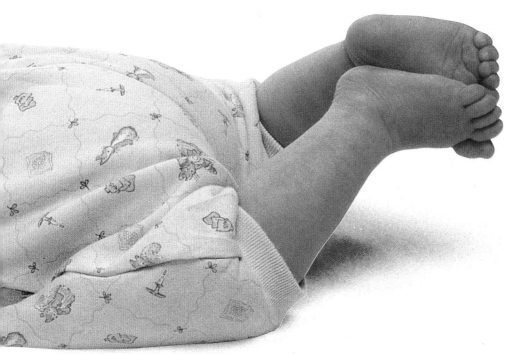

Your baby will now start to reach out for interesting toys and often try to put them in his mouth.

A young baby is fascinated by mirrors, but at distances she can only make out vague shapes.

If you place your baby 15–20 cm/6–8 in away from a mirror, she will be able to focus on her image and chat to herself.

that require chewing should not be introduced until your baby can sit up alone, which is not usually until about seven months.

First solids are little more than tasters that get a baby used to the idea of sucking from a spoon rather than from the breast or bottle. To be able to do this the tongue thrust reflex, which the baby was born with, must have disappeared. This is the reflex that causes the tongue to push any foreign matter out of the mouth and prevents very young babies from choking.

If the food offered is pushed straight back out of the mouth by the tongue and this happens several times, the reflex is still there and the baby is not ready for solids. To be able to eat from a spoon your baby also needs to be able to draw in his lower lip.

Another fairly obvious sign that your baby is ready for solids is if he shows any interest in the food that you are eating. If your baby watches intently while you eat and shows excitement or tries to grab your food, then he is probably telling you that he is now ready for more grown-up food himself. If you are unsure about when to start weaning your baby, remember to ask your doctor for advice.

THUMB SUCKING

Your baby will suck anything he can get into his mouth and now that he has some control over his hands, his fingers and thumbs will be preferred and he will suck them for pleasure and also for comfort. He may suck his whole hand, or one or two fingers, or he may prefer his thumb. This is quite normal and is not a sign of emotional distress, nor will it, at this age, damage the alignment of

permanent teeth. If your baby is breast-fed you need to make sure that he isn't sucking his thumb to compensate for suckling he is no longer getting at the breast; otherwise there is no harm if you let your child suck his thumb. Most children grow out of this habit naturally over the next year or two, although a child who uses sucking his thumb as reassurance to get to sleep may take a little longer to break the habit. This is nothing to worry about.

Immunization

At four months your baby will have the second immunizations for diphtheria, tetanus, whooping cough (DTP), Hib and polio.

You can now give some solids to your baby if she can hold her head upright and if food isn't rejected by her tongue.

Your baby will try to stand with help, but he shouldn't put too much weight on his legs.

FIVE MONTHS

Milestones

Your child may be able to:

- Hold her head steady when upright.
- Keep her head level with her body when pulled into the sitting position.
- Pay attention to a small object.
- Squeal with delight.
- Be able to say some vowel-consonant combinations such as "ah-coo".

Your baby's grasp of basic concepts is growing and she is thinking much faster. It is thought that a baby when she is first born will take between five and 10 minutes to get used to something new; by three months a baby may take between 30 seconds and two minutes and by six months she will take only 30 seconds.

Your baby will begin to learn about cause and effect by carrying out simple experiments, such as throwing a toy out of her pram. Initially she will believe that it has

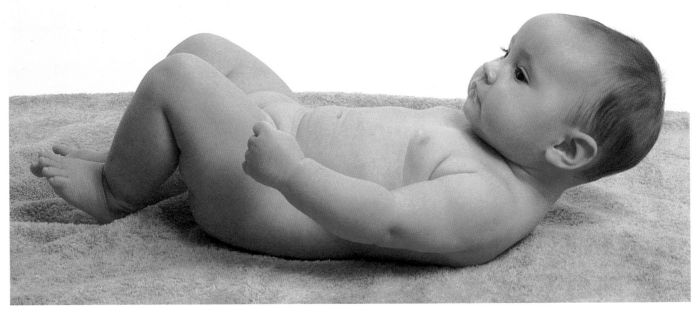

At five months, your baby will be able to lift her head up from a lying position and hold it steady.

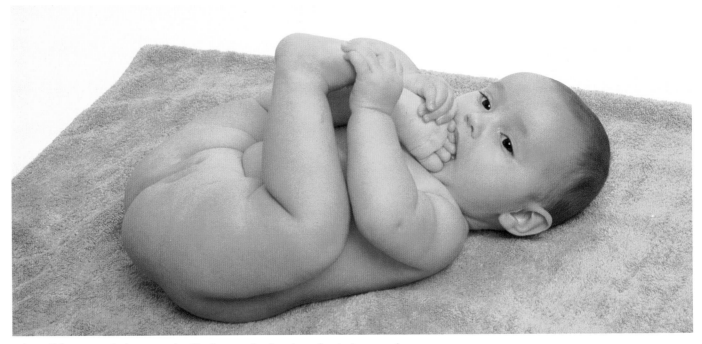

She will love to suck things, and will often put her hands or feet in her mouth.

Your baby's head movements are now getting much steadier as she gains more control.

vanished and won't understand where it has gone. If you pick up the toy and return it she will be both puzzled and delighted. She will do the trick again and again until she begins to realize that, by dropping the toy and getting it back, she is beginning to take control of her world by making things happen.

You can encourage your baby with her experiments by playing games such as peek-a-boo, or hiding an object that was in front of her and then making it reappear again. At this age your baby won't attempt to recover what you have hidden because she thinks that the object no longer exists because she can't see it.

It will be several months before she learns that this really isn't the case and starts looking for the hidden object herself.

TEETHING
There is no fixed time for your baby to start teething, but on average a baby's first tooth appears sometime

between now and seven months. Babies teethe differently, with some experiencing a lot of discomfort and others hardly seeming to notice their first teeth coming through. It is thought that tooth eruption follows hereditary patterns, so if you or your partner teethed especially early or late your baby may do the same.

Teething symptoms often precede the tooth itself by several weeks or even months, and vary from child to child. Drooling is often the first sign that teeth are on their way and this can start as early as 10 weeks. Excessive drooling can cause a dry skin rash or chapping on the chin and around the mouth, which should be treated with a mild skin cream. Biting is another indication of teething. Your baby may start chewing on anything she can get into her mouth as the counterpressure from chewing on a hard object helps relieve the pressure under the gums. Rubbing her gums with your finger may bring relief or you can give her something to chew on such as a chilled teething ring or a slice of carrot.

Delight your growing baby with different types of toys to keep her interested and fully stimulated.

Inflammation of the tender gum tissue often occurs when a tooth is coming through so your baby is likely to have red, sore gums before a tooth erupts. Ear pulling and cheek rubbing may also be a sign of teething as pain can travel along the nerve pathways to these areas. This is particularly common when the molars are coming through. If your child seems to be in pain you can give her the recommended dose of paracetamol. However, never attribute illnesses such as diarrhoea, fever, or earache to teething: if you are concerned seek medical advice.

Your baby will often prefer a simple toy like this rattle as it is easier for her to manage and play with.

SIX MONTHS

Your child is beginning to show a greater interest in what is going on around him. He will turn his head quickly to familiar voices and will examine things that interest him for longer periods.

THE BABY TAKES CONTROL

The baby is rapidly becoming more mobile and will probably be able to pull himself into the sitting position if both hands are held. When lying on his stomach, the baby may find that kicking will push him along, usually backwards at first. If he becomes frustrated because he can't get to where he wants to go, don't be too eager to help him. You can encourage him by placing a toy just out of reach, or by placing your hands against the soles of his feet so that when he kicks he has something to push against. If you pick him up and place him where he wants to go he will not learn how to achieve this for himself.

The baby's ability to reach and grasp is becoming more accurate and you can help him improve these skills by passing objects in such a way that he has to reach up or down or to the side for them. Toys strung across his cot or playpen will allow him to practise using these skills. Your baby will hold objects in the palm of his hands, and will be able to pass them from one hand to the other. You can encourage him by giving him two toys simultaneously, one in each hand, so that he has to reach out with both hands. If you offer him a rattle, shake it to make a noise as you hand it to him; he will reach for it immediately and then shake it deliberately to make the same noise.

Visually your baby is keenly aware of everything that is going on around him and will move his head and eyes eagerly in every direction to which his attention is attracted. He will follow what you are doing, even if you are busy on the other side of the room. His eyes now

Milestones

Your child may be able to:
- Laugh, chuckle, and squeal aloud and scream with annoyance.
- Use whole hand to grasp objects and can pass them from one hand to the other.
- Move his eyes in unison and turn his head and eyes towards something that attracts him.
- Play with his feet as well as his hands.
- Can manipulate small objects.
- Start to be wary of strangers.

Right and opposite: If you have a very active baby it is best not to put her in her high chair at meal times until her food is ready to eat or has cooled, as she will only get restless and may have a temper tantrum because she can't easily move around. A quieter baby will probably be quite happy to sit in her chair and play for a while with a stimulating toy that you have given her. If she is content to sit quietly and amuse herself until you can feed her, it will also give you peace of mind that she is safe and not getting into any other mischief as you prepare her food and drink.

move in unison so if your child appears to be cross-eyed (with an eye turned inward or outward all the time) he should see an eye specialist.

If your baby drops a toy within his field of vision he will watch until it reaches its resting place. Toys falling outside his visual field will be ignored or forgotten.

Your child is now very chatty and will vocalize tunefully both to himself and others in a singsong manner using vowel sounds and single and double syllables such as "a-a," "adah" and "er-leh." He laughs, chuckles, and squeals with delight when playing and will express anger or annoyance with loud screams.

INTELLIGENCE

Assessing a child's IQ (intelligence quotient) when he is very young is difficult, and the motor development tests that can be used to evaluate IQ in the first year do not usually correlate well with a child's IQ later on. Intelligence can be influenced by many factors, including stimulation, health and diet as well as social aspects such as poverty. Even trauma can play a part. At this stage in your child's development you can encourage his physical, social, and intellectual growth by raising him in a stimulating environment and spending time playing, reading, and talking to him.

It is hard to predict how fast your baby will develop, but she will be stimulated by your talking and playing with her.

Always buy toys that suit the age of your baby. This one has bendable projections that he can easily grasp.

Once you have helped your baby to sit up, she will often sit quite happily and watch you as you move around the room.

SEVEN MONTHS

Learning to move from one place to another is a huge achievement for your baby and one which will give her a whole new perspective on the world. How this locomotion is achieved will vary from baby to baby. Some crawl on all fours, others creep by wriggling on their fronts, others roll their way from one place to another. Some push themselves backwards, which can be very frustrating for them. It is thought that the children who walk the earliest are those who have crawled first or those who have gone straight from sitting to standing. Bottom shufflers and creepers tend to walk a bit later. However, there is little to suggest that a crawler who becomes an early walker is any brighter than a creeper who walks a little later.

Your baby will be able to take some weight on her legs now and she may even be able to stand while you hold her in an upright position. Over the next couple of months she will probably learn to pull herself up from sitting, and then she will practise standing alone.

At seven months your baby will be able to sit up and turn at the waist. She will also like to suck her thumb.

Your baby is developing a mind of her own and will often try to wriggle free when picked up or held.

DEXTERITY

Your baby may start to show a preference for using her right or left hand at this age. Offer her a toy held straight in front of her and see which hand she uses to reach for it. If your baby regularly uses the same hand she is beginning to show a preference, but this is by no means a final choice. Very often the hand she uses at seven months is not the same as the one she prefers at nine months

Milestones

Your child may be able to:

• Put weight on legs when upright.

• Sit with minimal support.

• Look for a dropped object.

• Babble combining vowels and consonants such as "ga-ga", "ma-ma" and "da-da".

• Feed herself with finger foods.

• Begin to crawl.

Your baby is now very much on the move and will be beginning to crawl everywhere quite quickly.

Your baby will hold toys in both hands with much more dexterity now. She will also still enjoy sucking them.

Try and talk to your baby as much as you can as he will reply with babble that mixes both vowels and consonants.

or a year. Once your baby is able to use two hands in a coordinated way, give her something which needs one hand to hold it and another to make it work – a pot with a lid that comes off is ideal – and see which hand she uses for which action. This will give you a better idea of whether your baby is likely to be left- or right-handed, although her final choice may not be made until she reaches two years of age.

You may notice that your baby no longer grasps things in the centre of her palm to hold them. She now uses her fingers and thumb so that her grip has become very much more refined. Now that she can operate her fingers and thumb independently, rather than using them as a rake, she can pick up an object as small as a raisin to examine it.

You can encourage the baby by allowing her to feed herself. Give her a bowl and spoon and let her get on with it. At first it is a good idea for you to have a spoon too, so that you can give her the occasional mouthful while she is still working out how to get the food from the

bowl, onto the spoon and into her mouth. Finger foods will help your baby learn how to get food into her mouth using her fingers.

At around the time your baby starts to show hand preference her language also starts to become more fully developed and she will babble a lot more using both vowel sounds and consonants. Her cries also change to include both low- and high-pitched sounds and she will start to make different movements with her tongue and mouth.

As his hand movements improve, your baby will start to grasp toys, such as bricks, with his fingers and thumb.

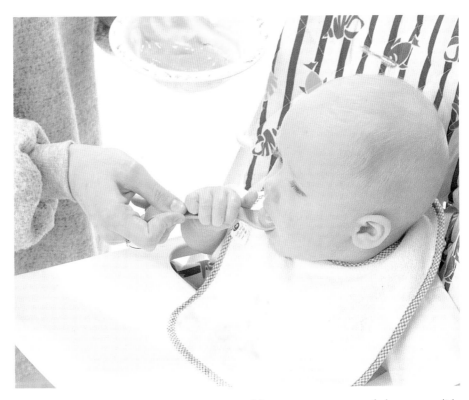

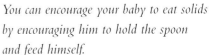

You can encourage your baby to eat solids by encouraging him to hold the spoon and feed himself.

EIGHT MONTHS

By eight months your baby will probably have started to be selective about the people with whom he is sociable. The outgoing friendliness of the earlier months may have been replaced by a certain wariness, especially of strangers. If you leave your baby with someone he doesn't know he may now burst into tears, whereas before he would have been perfectly happy, as long as he was being entertained and was warm and comfortable. This new-found wariness of strangers often occurs at about the same time that your baby is making a surge in his development. About a month after this, your baby may start to show distress, sometimes known as separation anxiety, when you leave the room. This distress at being separated from you or your partner will probably peak at around 15 months and then gradually subside.

If your baby does suffer from separation anxiety it can be misery for both of you. The best way of easing his distress is to leave him in a familiar environment with, if possible, a well-known person or relative.

Favourite and familiar toys can also be a source of comfort.

When you are leaving your baby to go out, try to leave quickly without making a fuss and keep your goodbyes down to a minimum.

As the bond grows stronger between you and your child, he will appreciate as much attention as you can give him.

Milestones

Your child may be able to:

• Stand up while holding onto something firmly.

• Get himself into a sitting position from his stomach.

• Pick up a small object with his hand such as a raisin.

• Turn round in the direction of a familiar voice.

• Move himself towards an out-of-reach toy.

DISCOVERING GENITALS

It is normal for your baby to start to show an interest in his genitals at around this age. This interest is an inevitable and healthy part of your baby's development in the same way that his fascination with his fingers and toes was earlier. There is no harm, either physical or psychological, in your baby handling his genitals and you should never make your child feel bad or think about punishing him because he is doing so.

A boy is capable of having an erection from before birth; this is simply the normal response to the touch of a sensitive organ. A baby girl has clitoral erections from a very young age too, although these are much less obvious.

INTRODUCING BOOKS

From eight months onwards, your baby's behaviour will become more flexible and he will begin to use his own initiative in a relationship. He will give you toys as well as taking them and may even start playing simple games with you. For the first time he will want to share his interest in an object with another person. This is a good time to introduce him to books which you can sit and read together. At first he will only be interested in the rhythm and sound of the words and the colour and pattern of the pictures in the book. By speaking slowly in a singsong manner, putting exaggerated emphasis in the right places, and encouraging your child to join in with simple sounds such as "moo" when he sees the picture of a cow, you will make reading a shared, enjoyable experience.

DEVELOPMENTAL CHECK

At between six and nine months your baby will be given another developmental check by your doctor

Your baby will happily respond to your games and will often try playful actions like grabbing your hair.

Left: As the grasping action is much more developed, your child will enjoy handling and playing with stacking toys. He may need guidance from you as to the order the shapes go in, and which colour should go next.

Opposite: A car or any toy with wheels is likely to be a particular source of interest for your baby. He may just want to sit and play with it, and only go after it if you join in and spend time pushing it back and forth to him.

or health visitor. She will be looking to see how your baby is developing and also checking that nothing has been missed in any previous health checks. Your baby's pelvis and legs will be examined to make sure there is no congenital dislocation of the hips. If your baby is a boy his testicles will be checked to make sure they are well down in the scrotum. A distraction test for hearing will be carried out. This involves making a noise for two seconds with something like a bell or rattle out of your baby's sight to see whether he turns towards the sound. His eyes will be checked to see that there is no sign of a potential squint. You will probably be asked if your baby has ever had any breathing problems such as wheezing, and his heart and lungs may be checked with a stethoscope. He may be weighed and his height measured and the circumference of his head checked.

If you are worried about any part of your child's development you should talk about your concerns now with your doctor. The health visitor or doctor will be able to help with any questions you may have and can also offer advice if you are experiencing problems with feeding your child or with his sleeping.

NINE MONTHS

A nine-month-old baby is capable of showing a wide range of emotions from happiness to fear, anger, and sadness and she will use these as a means of expressing feelings at any given moment. Your child needs you to be in tune with her feelings and to understand what she is trying to express, otherwise she will become frustrated and unhappy. She may begin to show signs of early independence, but she will still want the reassurance of knowing that you are nearby and ready to help out if required.

MOVEMENT

Your baby can now sit alone for 10–15 minutes at a time and will be able to lean forward to pick up a toy without falling over. She can also turn her body and will stretch out for something at her side. She will spend time manipulating a toy with her hands and is able to pass the toy from one hand to the other, turning it as she does so. She uses a pincer grasp, using her finger and thumb, to pick up small items. She will poke at things with a forefinger and may even start to point. You will notice that she still cannot put down a toy she is holding. She will still drop it or press it against a hard surface to release it. If she drops a toy she will look where it has fallen, even if it has completely disappeared from view.

Your child is now very active and she will begin to move herself

Your baby is now constantly on the move and will use her hands to help push her forward as she crawls along.

As she moves along she will be distracted if you call out her name, and might even topple over as her balance is still unsteady.

As she pushes forward with her arms, her legs will move back and forth to propel her along.

Milestones

Your child may be able to:

• Look for an object that she dropped out of view.

• Pull herself into a standing position.

• Pick up small objects using her finger and thumb.

• Enjoy games such as pat-a-cake.

• Wave goodbye.

• Cruise around the furniture.

across the floor either by crawling, or by shuffling or rolling if she can't yet crawl. She will try pulling herself to standing while holding onto something and may manage to hold herself upright for a few moments before sitting down with a bump. She won't be able to lower herself in a controlled way into a sitting position. If you hold her in a standing position she will probably make purposeful stepping movements with alternate feet as though she is practising walking.

ACTIVITY

You will notice that your child is becoming a lot more vocal now. She will shout for your attention, stop, listen for your response, and, if she doesn't get it, she will shout again. She will hold long conversations with you, babbling in a loud, tuneful way using strings of syllables such as "dad-da", "ma-ma", "aga-aga", over and over again. She not only uses this babble as a means of interpersonal communication to show friendliness or annoyance, but also as

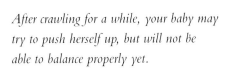

After crawling for a while, your baby may try to push herself up, but will not be able to balance properly yet.

a way of amusing herself. She likes to practise imitating adult sounds, not just talking but also smacking her lips, coughing and making "brrr"-type noises.

By now your baby will be able to bite and chew her food well and she will be able to feed herself with some finger foods. She will probably try to grasp hold of the spoon as she is being fed. Let her have her own play spoon so that she can continue to practise feeding herself between the mouthfuls of food you are giving to her.

Your baby will probably enjoy games such as "peek-a-boo" and looking for something that you've half hidden while she watched. She will be delighted when she discovers the item and will show it to you with great glee. You may even be able to get her to look for something that you've completely hidden, but she won't necessarily be able to find it and this may cause her some distress and even annoyance.

If your baby seems at all worried by these first simple games you will need to encourage her to take part in them by responding to all her efforts with obvious surprise or

All toys will be held firmly now by your baby, who will use a pincer grasp with her finger and thumb.

Your baby's fascination with her toes will continue and she will often be found playing with them.

Right: As bonding with her father continues, your baby will enjoy being lifted up in the air and other games with him.

delight. She will be happy when you show her how much you enjoy her cleverness because she will enjoy your approval.

As your baby starts to become more confident, the games to play will become more adventurous. She will let you know when she is ready to progress to the next stage.

Below: Your baby will not play with an older brother at this stage, but she will be interested in toys he is showing her.

Standing up will be a problem unless there is a support nearby. If he lets go he will sit down with a bump.

TEN MONTHS

You will probably have discovered by now that your child has a sense of humour. At 10 months, your baby will not only enjoy playing games with you but will also rock with laughter at some of his own antics. For example, he will enjoy splashing in the bath and this will become even more fun if he gets you wet too. The more you protest the more he will enjoy splashing you. You may also find some of the things you do make your baby laugh uproariously. Appearing around a door saying "boo" can make him squeal with laughter and he will enjoy this game over and over again. Your baby may also enjoy teasing you in return by offering you a toy and then snatching it back before you can take it.

Traditional nursery rhymes and games can give your child endless fun. Try saying: "Round and round the garden, like a teddy bear, one step, two step, tickly under there!" as you run your fingers around his palm, then up his arm and end with a tickle. Another favourite is Humpty Dumpty. Build up to a climax at the point Humpty is going to fall off the wall and pretend to let

Milestones

Your child may be able to:

• Move around the furniture.

• Understand the word "no", but not necessarily obey it.

• Stand alone for a few seconds.

• Use the word "dada" to get his father's attention.

• Hold a feeder cup to drink from it.

• Roll a ball back to you.

Your child is now developing rapidly and will be trying to stand. He won't be able to do it on his own and will need your support.

He might try a few faltering steps, but can't easily manage these and will need to hold onto one of your hands as he moves forwards.

Supports, such as a chair, will be used by your child to pull himself up as he learns to stand.

your baby fall too. The baby has probably reached what is sometimes known as the joint-attention stage. This is when a child is able to concentrate on more than one thing at a time. You can encourage this by pointing out things while also giving your baby some information. For example, you can show your child a cat, then tell him that when a cat speaks it says "miaow". Later, when he sees a cat again, you can ask him what the cat says. This is a great way of sharing knowledge and making learning fun.

ESTABLISHING ROLES

Along with this sense of humour, new mobility, and the desire to share with you, comes a real talent for getting into trouble. Your baby's curiosity will lead him into all sorts of dangers and you will need to be constantly on your guard so that he isn't allowed to hurt himself. Your baby, on the other hand, may see thwarting your efforts at keeping

him out of mischief as a great way of getting a response from you. For the first time since your child was born you may begin to think about using some form of discipline.

Discipline doesn't mean rules and punishment, it means teaching the concept of right and wrong. It will be a long time before your child fully grasps the idea of what is involved, but by teaching him now, through your example and guidance, you will be helping him towards eventual self-control and showing him that he needs to have respect for other people.

It is important to remember that a baby cannot be bad because babies and toddlers do not know right from wrong. They learn about their world through experimentation, and by observing and testing adults. Introducing the concept of things being right or wrong at this early age is the first step to helping your child develop from a naturally self-centred baby to a much more sensitive and

caring child. The most effective discipline is neither uncompromisingly rigid nor too permissive. Either of these extremes can leave a child feeling unloved.

You need to set limits and standards that are fair and enforce them firmly, but lovingly. Never threaten to withdraw love from your child as this will badly effect his self-esteem and it is important that he knows he is loved even when you don't approve of his behaviour.

Don't smack your child. Smacking has been shown not to be an effective way to discipline a naughty child. It has many negative aspects including teaching the child violence and that using force is the best way of ending a dispute or getting what you want.

Opposite: A container with various slots for different shapes will keep a child amused as he tries to work out which one should go in the right hole.

A young baby will use a low stool for support as he moves around.

If a stool is at the right level, your baby may use it as a means of pulling himself up, and as a table to leave some of his toys there in easy reach.

ELEVEN MONTHS

Many babies speak their first word at around 11 months, although some speak as early as nine months and others don't say a word until well after a year. This is a remarkable achievement when you consider that not very long ago your child didn't even know how to smile. These first words take the longest to learn and you will need to be patient while you wait for your child to produce another new one. Sometimes these first words are learned as infrequently as one a month from now on, until your child has a vocabulary of around 10 words. After this the rate usually increases quickly, but this stage isn't reached until around 15 months of age.

DEVELOPING SPEECH

You can help your child to build up her vocabulary by saying the names of things in which she expresses an interest. By now she can probably point at items that she wants because she will have already discovered that pointing is an effective means of communicating with you. When you pick up the item and hand it to the child you probably tell her what

Milestones

Your child may be able to:
• Say the word "mama" to attract your attention.
• Stand on her own.
• Take her first steps.
• Respond to a simple command which isn't accompanied by gestures.
• Say her first word other than "mama" and "dada".

At 11 months your child will be much more responsive and will start reacting to simple questions and commands.

it is. For example, your child points at an apple, you pick up the apple and hand it to her saying something like: "You want this apple?" By doing this you are teaching your child new words; although she may not remember them straightaway, in time each word will become part of her vocabulary.

Don't worry if you are the only person who can understand your baby's first words. It is not unusual for others outside the family to be baffled by the way a baby speaks. It may well be two or three years before your child can be easily understood outside the immediate family. It is important not to keep correcting your child's pronunciation.

This will knock her confidence and she may become worried about trying to use new words. However, don't revert to using her wrongly pronounced words simply because they sound really cute. If you imitate her errors, the child will carry on using the incorrect words for much longer than she would otherwise have done.

MOBILITY

Your baby may have started to pull herself up onto her feet; she may even be walking by holding onto the furniture. Don't be tempted to rush out and buy shoes at the first sign of walking because the child doesn't need shoes yet, in fact they would

not be good for her feet at this stage. A child needs to wear shoes when she is walking confidently and her feet will need protection when she goes outside.

Learning to walk is a matter of trial and error. You can't really do anything to help your child apart from making sure that the area she is learning to walk in is as safe as possible. But even when you have removed all the obvious hazards in your child's path you need to stay close at hand to make sure that she doesn't hurt herself.

A child is bound to experience falls while mastering the art of walking and your reaction to these mishaps can colour your child's

ur developing baby will now start to share things and will happily hand you s, such as a ball.

Even though she now has some teeth, your baby will still like the sensation of putting different objects in her mouth.

Right: Your baby will be particularly responsive playing games now. If you keep hiding a toy and then making it re-appear it will keep her happily amused for quite a while.

Below left and right: Your child will enjoy standing upright with some help from you. Provided she can hang onto something with one hand, she will eagerly pick up toys from the floor to show you, wave around or suck.

response to them as well. If you rush over in a panic every time she stumbles and demand to know if she is all right she may well shed more tears than she would if she'd really hurt herself. This over-reaction on your part may also make her lose her sense of adventure and make her afraid of attempting other normal physical development hurdles. By remaining calm and reacting with an "up you get, you're all right" sort of attitude, your child is likely to deal with minor tumbles in a matter-of-fact way.

Left: By pushing a baby walker, your baby can walk happily around the room. Keep an eye on her so that you can help if she gets stuck in a corner. It takes time for a child to learn how to walk backwards. Below: A child will place her favourite toys on a low-level table and play with them there. When she is bored she may just leave them and go off to do something else more interesting.

TWELVE MONTHS

You are the parent of a year-old child. One by one all the skills that will make your baby a self-dependent and integrated member of society are being perfected. You are both teacher and observer. And now the changes come very quickly indeed.

GROWING SKILLS

If your baby isn't actually walking he should be well on his way to doing so by the end of the first year. He will probably be able to pull himself to his feet and navigate by holding onto the furniture. He will certainly be crawling, bottom shuffling, or rolling, and he will be able to get around at quite some speed. He will be able to sit for long periods and can now get into the sitting position from lying flat.

Your baby's grasp is now more refined and he will be able to pick up small objects using the thumb and the tip of the index finger. He will drop and throw toys deliberately and enjoy watching them as they fall. If a toy rolls out of sight he may look for it. He uses both hands to hold toys, but he may start to show a preference for using one hand rather than the other. When your child wants to show you something he will point using his index finger. He's curious and will want to explore everything, so make sure that your home is a safe place. This doesn't mean restricting your baby to such an extent that he becomes frustrated. Try to compromise by leaving some safe cupboards for him to get into and locking the others.

When the baby is outside he will watch people, animals, or cars with prolonged, intent regard. He will be able to recognize familiar people or animals from around 6 m/20 ft and will probably greet them vocally with great enthusiasm. The child responds to his own name and can understand other words such as the

Milestones

Your child may be able to:
• Indicate what he wants in other ways instead of crying.
• Stand on his own.
• Walk a little way unaided.
• Wave goodbye to you, close relatives and friends.
• Say "mama" and "dada" with discrimination.
• Roll a ball back to you.

At 12 months your child will be able to let you know what he wants by pointing or reaching towards an object.

All children vary when they first start walking, but your child may well be taking his first few steps now, so you should give him every encouragement.

names of family members. He may be able to understand simple instructions such as "give it to Mummy", and he may even do as you ask.

You may find that your baby holds out his arm or leg when you ask him to while you are bathing or dressing him. You will see through his actions that he can understand much of what you say even though he can't yet express himself verbally. He babbles to himself and to you, making a lot of speech-type sounds and if he hasn't already said his first word then he soon will.

Eating habits

Your baby will be joining in family meals and will probably be eating a mashed-up version of whatever everyone else eats. He is still too young to eat spicy or seasoned food, so remove his portion before adding salt and pepper and other seasoning. He enjoys finger foods but will want to imitate others at mealtimes by using a spoon. It will be difficult for him to get food onto the spoon and then the spoon into his mouth, so he may well revert to using his fingers after a few attempts.

Your child will be able to drink from a feeder cup by himself and will probably be able to drink from an ordinary cup with your help, but he's still too young to manage this on his own. If you are weaning, or are about to wean your baby off his bottle or the breast, you may want to start giving him cows' milk as his main drink. This should only be introduced into your baby's diet after the age of one year and you should always give him whole, pasteurized milk. Skimmed milk has too much protein and sodium content for babies and should not be introduced into your child's diet before the age

of five. Semi-skimmed milk can be given from two years, but only if the child is eating a very varied and adequate diet.

Your baby may be reluctant to give up the bottle because it may be a source of emotional comfort, but it is recommended that a child stops drinking from a bottle at around a year because of the adverse effect it can have on his teeth. If you don't feel that he is ready to give up his bottle completely, try to limit the number of times he has a bottle each day. Encourage him to drink from a trainer cup at meal times and offer

him a bottle between meals and at bedtime. When you give a bottle during the day, fill it with water rather than juice or milk, because this will help reduce your child's interest in it. Insist that he drinks from it while sitting in an adult's lap and when he wants to get down take the bottle from him. Don't allow him to take his bottle to bed or to walk about with it. By restricting the use of a bottle like this you will limit the amount of potential harm it can do to his teeth.

Your baby may have as many as four or five teeth and you should

Toys such as a cuddly, soft panda will soon become a firm favourite with your child as he will enjoy its furry texture.

When your child has a favourite cuddly animal he will love to carry it around, hug and squeeze it, and may want to take it with him wherever he goes.

have been cleaning them from the time they appeared. These first teeth can be cleaned with a soft baby toothbrush and a pea-sized amount of children's toothpaste. If your baby is cutting teeth and is fretful, offer him a cold teething ring or a piece of raw carrot to chew on.

YOUR CHILD AND OTHERS

Even though he is confident and outgoing with you, your baby may still be wary of strangers. He may also suffer from shyness. This is an inherited trait which he will have got from either you or your partner, even though neither of you may appear to display the trait yourselves. Shyness can be modified, but it is rarely possible to eradicate it altogether. If you build up your child's confidence with praise and encouragement

this will help him to feel more comfortable with others and this may eventually help diminish any shyness.

It is possible that what you consider to be shyness is actually just a normal lack of sociability. At this age your child is not ready to make friends, and he probably won't be until he is at least three years old. Until then the social limit will probably be parallel play, which is when he plays side by side with another child. Don't try to force your child to play with others – pushing him may make him withdraw from social situations completely.

Don't expect a child to share his toys at this age. Right now the only things that matter are his own needs and desires. Other children are seen as objects not people. If he displays aggressive behaviour towards other children, like biting or hitting, you need to respond immediately by removing him from the scene of the incident. Explain calmly why he shouldn't have behaved like that, then give him something to play with or point out a new object to distract him and change the subject. Of course he won't really understand what you are saying but, if you use this approach every time it happens, he will eventually understand that hitting and biting other people are just not acceptable behaviour.

Opposite: *Although your child will be perfectly happy when being held by you, he may be shy and withdrawn with other people he doesn't know.*
Below: *Your baby will interact quite happily with his father and will keep experimenting with touch.*

UNDERSTANDING YOUR CHILD'S DEVELOPMENT

SIGHT AND VISION

Although your baby practised the blinking reflex by opening and closing her eyes while she was in the womb, the first time she actually uses her eyes for seeing is at the moment of birth. As soon as she is born she is capable of distinguishing objects and most colours; but she is only able to focus on items that are 20–30 cm/ 8–12 in away. These things will look slightly fuzzy and be lacking in definition and, since the images from the retinas of the eyes haven't merged yet, your baby's world will appear as if seen through two separate tunnels.

A newborn is very sensitive to bright lights and will blink and screw up her eyes if a light is shone in her face. Movement will attract a baby from birth and you may notice that yours actively seeks out moving objects. She will probably show a preference for an object which has a highly contrasting pattern rather than one which is just a solid block of colour. As your baby begins to control her eye movements she will start tracking moving objects, and it is then that her eyes will begin to start working together.

YOUR BABY'S WORLD

At first your face will be of more interest to your child than anything else. It is thought that a baby is born with a simple mental template of the human face and will actively search out and stare at any human face during the first couple of months. When she is first born, whether she is able to recognize you by your individual features is open to debate, but she will certainly know the general shape of your head and hairline and by two months will have started to recognize your features.

Your baby will soon become interested in other things and by six to eight weeks she will be concentrating on details, scanning faces and

A newborn baby's vision will be fairly limited and initially he will only be able to see a fuzzy image of you.

objects so that she can take in as much information as possible. At this age she may find it hard to disengage her attention when she is watching something and she may need you to distract her before she can remove her gaze. But by three to four months the pathways in the brain for voluntary action begin to take over and your baby starts to disengage her attention on her own.

By three months a baby can perceive colours fully, with all their different shades, and will be able to focus at different distances and to see things in 3D. From seven to eight months as

Your young baby will become fascinated by different objects and will become difficult to distract from whatever is capturing her attention.

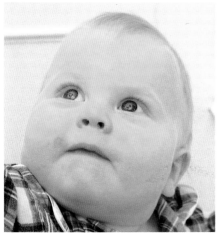

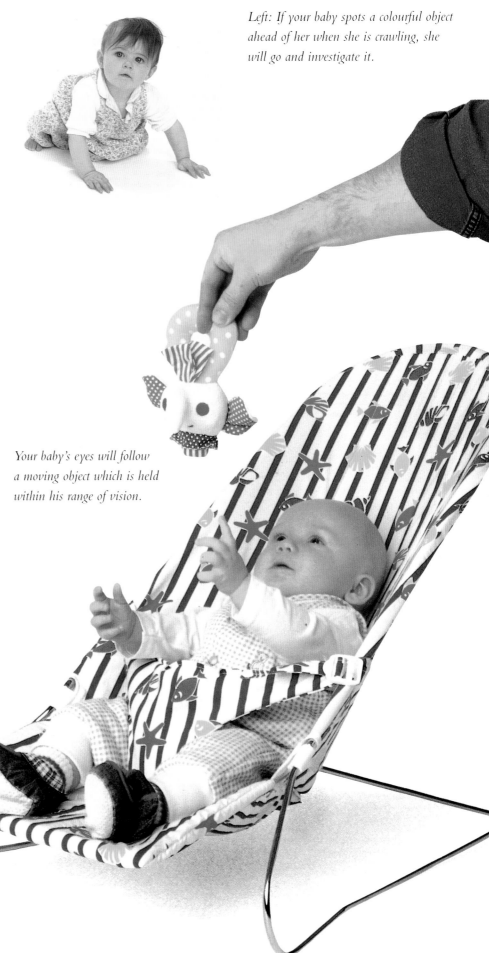

Left: If your baby spots a colourful object ahead of her when she is crawling, she will go and investigate it.

Your baby's eyes will follow a moving object which is held within his range of vision.

As your baby's eyesight improves, he will intently watch everything that is going on around him (top and above).

she begins to interpret what she sees, your baby starts to realize that things don't necessarily cease to exist just because she can't see them anymore. A toy dropped over the edge of the high chair will be looked for; she will also enjoy playing "peek-a-boo" because she knows now that you will definitely reappear.

Learning the size and shape of things and understanding that something that looks small at a distance is in fact the same size close up takes some time for a baby to understand. She will also have to learn that a toy stays the same shape even when it appears

How you can help

• Give your baby plenty of stimulating things to look at.

• Hold an item within her range of vision and move it slowly in an arc so that she can follow it with her eyes.

• Play games like "peek-a-boo" and "hide-and-seek" with a toy or by hiding under a large cloth or blanket.

• Check that your child doesn't have a squint. If you are concerned, talk to your doctor.

different when looked at from the side, top, or bottom. It will take your baby around two years to have good vision and to be able to see as clearly as an adult does.

A SQUINT

Many babies are born with what may appear to be a slight squint and this often remains until they have learned to control the muscles around the eyes. It is quite difficult for a baby to hold both eyes in line with each other to focus on an object, and you may notice that when your baby stares at you one of her eyes wanders out of focus. A wandering eye usually rights itself by the time a baby reaches six months old, but you should always point it out to your doctor or health visitor as it may be necessary for your child's eyes to be checked thoroughly by a specialist.

A real squint is when the eyes never focus together on an object and, rather than moving together and then one wandering off, they are often out of alignment with each other. A squint needs to be treated from an early age so you must talk to your doctor as soon as you notice it in your child.

A brightly coloured mobile, moving in the breeze and suspended or held from above, will delight your child and keep him amused for a long time.

HEARING

During the last three months in the uterus a baby will have been hearing a variety of different noises. By the time a baby is born, he will already be familiar with his mother's voice, the beating of her heart, and the sound of the amniotic fluid in which he has been floating. His ability to hear at birth is almost as good as an adult's. His hearing threshold, however, is lower so your baby will be startled by loud, unfamiliar noises, although he will probably sleep happily through a constant loud sound such as a blaring television or loud music.

A very young baby will prefer to hear rhythmic noises that may not seem soothing to you: the noise of a washing machine or tumble dryer, the hum of the vacuum cleaner or hair dryer. These will probably reassure him and may even lull him to sleep, perhaps because he heard such sounds before birth and he finds them both comforting and familiar.

Your own child will quickly associate you and your voice with comfort – it is thought that an infant of only a few days old can actually recognize his mother's voice. Your baby will respond to all the human voices he hears and will turn towards the sound of people talking and appear to listen intently. If he is being spoken to in the exaggerated, high-pitched tone, and rhythmic singsong manner, known as "motherese" that adults often instinctively adopt for babies, you will notice that your baby pays particular attention. He may even lose interest if the speaker reverts to a normal tone.

It is through hearing others speak that your baby will eventually learn to form the words which will make up early vocabulary. He will start to understand what is being said long before he can actually make the noises himself; if he has a hearing defect this knowledge and the eventual ability to speak will be affected. As your baby gets older he will start looking for the source of the different sounds that he hears and will respond with obvious pleasure to familiar voices, words, and tunes.

HEARING TESTS

At your baby's first developmental check, at between six and eight weeks, your doctor will want to know whether you have any concerns about your baby's hearing and

How you can help

- When the baby is very young, try not to let him become startled by sudden noises which make him cry.
- Talk to your child, using "motherese", the high-pitched, singsong voice that babies find appealing.
- Introduce him to many different sounds from an early age.
- Let him sleep where he is happiest rather than insisting that he should be in a quiet room on his own.

From an early age your baby will respond to your voice and be interested in toys you are showing him.

He will turn towards any new or interesting noise that you make with a toy even if it is coming from behind him.

how he responds to your voice at home. You should mention if there is a close family history of hearing problems. If there is any concern, your baby can be referred to a hearing clinic.

At eight or nine months, your baby will have his next developmental check and this will include a screening test of your baby's hearing carried out by your health visitor. By now the response to sounds should be obvious, turning his head when you speak to him and responding to different noises of varying pitch and intensity. Both ears will be tested to identify anything previously missed.

If your child is deaf or partially deaf, his speech may not progress past the babbling stage and you may notice that he becomes quieter as he gets older. Any concerns about your child's hearing should be discussed with your doctor as soon as they occur.

Your baby will study your expression and listen intently to your voice before trying to imitate you.

SMELL, TASTE, TOUCH

SMELL

Newborn babies are very sensitive to smell and can remember certain smells almost from the moment they are born. They recognize their parents' natural smell and a breast-fed baby can distinguish the smell of her mother's milk from that of any other woman's just a few hours after birth. In fact, your baby will start sucking in her sleep if she smells your milk.

A bottle-fed baby will quickly learn to identify her own mother's smell and the smell of any other family members who also feed her. The smell of people who are familiar to her will help your baby distinguish between family members and people strange to her.

As your baby grows, certain smells will become associated with specific things, just as they do for adults. For example, food smells will suggest mealtimes and perhaps happy social occasions, while the smell of bath preparation and baby powder will become associated with bathtime and bed. Smells that your baby finds unpleasant will make her turn her head away even when she is only a few days old.

Your baby will use her sense of smell with her other senses to learn about the world around her.

From a young age, a baby has a highly developed sense of smell and she will delight in a sweet-smelling flower.

Taste is very important to a baby and she will experiment with the sensation of sucking her toys.

From the moment he is born, your baby will be able to react to bitter tastes and show a preference for sweet foods.

How you can help

• Spend time cuddling and talking to your baby so that she really gets to know you.

• Offer your child a wide variety of tastes once she is old enough to take solids, but avoid foods that are seasoned or spicy.

• Don't encourage your child to have a sweet tooth.

• Remember that a young baby cannot control her temperature as well as an older child, so you need to keep a constant check on her to make sure she isn't too cold or if she is becoming overheated.

• Your baby's skin is very sensitive so check that her clothes aren't tight or rubbing her skin.

TASTE

Smell and taste are intrinsically linked so it is no surprise that a baby is born with the ability to differentiate between tastes. From birth your baby's taste buds can detect sweet, sour, bitter, and salty. When offered any of these tastes she will give a definite and consistent reaction to each one. Her taste buds will become more refined with age, but even as a newborn baby she will show appreciation for sweet flavours and grimace when experiencing salty or bitter tastes.

All babies seem to be born with a preference for a sweeter taste, probably because breast milk is slightly sweet and it is important that she likes its flavour. This natural preference for sweet things won't harm your baby's teeth providing that you don't indulge her by giving her sweetened juice to drink, or adding sugar to her food when you start to wean her. When you start to introduce solids into your baby's diet it is better to encourage her to eat bland foods at first and then savoury foods and to keep sweet things to a minimum. Your baby will quickly develop her own tastes and you can help by giving her a varied diet once she is old enough to take solids.

By the time your child is around a year old she will use her experience of the different foods she has tried to help her distinguish between the more subtle flavours. For example, one brand of baked beans will taste slightly different to another and at a year old your child will be able to taste the difference.

TOUCH

Your baby uses touch immediately after birth. This provides her with a means of finding out about her new environment through the textures that her skin comes into contact with, like her clothes, your clothes, and skin. Your baby can also feel through her skin whether her environment is warm or cold, wet or dry. She feels pain and discomfort and, because a young baby has more sensitive skin than an adult, you need to treat her gently.

As she matures, your baby will use touch in different ways to help her learn. Touch-sensitive nerve endings are concentrated at the end of the fingertips and around the lips, and a young baby will use her hands and mouth for exploring new objects. Gradually, after a few weeks touch will also become associated with feelings and your baby will start to connect the feeling of your nipple in her mouth or your arms around her and associate them with warmth and security. One of the most important sensory experiences for your baby is through her tongue and mouth so that sucking is not only a means of obtaining nourishment, but is also

Your young baby will reach out and touch different objects, such as this furry panda, to get used to the different sensations.

a great source of comfort for her.

When you undress your baby you may notice that she becomes increasingly tense as you remove each layer of clothes and she may actually cry when you remove the garment nearest to her skin, usually her vest. This is not because you are being clumsy, but because she physically misses the feel of her clothes against her skin. She should stop crying as soon as you dress her again.

Between two and three months your child begins to use touch as a means of exploring and she will use her hands to hit out at things that are near her. By around five months she will have mastered hand and eye co-ordination and will learn by feeling and putting things in her mouth.

BONDING

Touch plays an important part in the main bonding process. This is the formation of a close emotional relationship between you and your baby which will provide her with the love, comfort, and security that she wants. Although your baby is born with a deep-rooted psychological need to have a close interaction with you this doesn't always happen immediately. A child's bonding with her mother is often a gradual process which may not be fully completed until the baby is a few months old.

At a few months old a young baby will react to bright toys such as this octopus which has two different materials on the undersides of its legs. He will enjoy the feel of soft textures.

TALKING

Your child is born with the potential to learn to speak and a receptiveness to the influences that will help him communicate. A baby starts to learn about language while he is still in the womb, which is when he first begins to identify the voice of his mother. As a newborn he will prefer his mother's voice to any other because it will already be familiar and he will quickly associate it with warmth, comfort, and feeding. A newborn baby's brain is tuned to pick out the texture, pattern, and rhythm of language and he will pay more attention to voices talking than any other sounds he hears. From the moment he is born your baby understands speech sounds in a way that allows him to segment the speech he hears into sound units.

Before he can speak fluently a baby has to go through distinct stages of development. In the beginning your baby's vocal skills will consist of cries and burps. The inability to speak in the early months does not actually hinder a baby's ability to become a talker. He uses this time to learn how to control his mouth and his tongue. You may notice that from a very early age your baby will move his mouth a lot, pushing his lips forwards and backwards in a kind of rhythm.

Conversations

One of the skills your baby has to acquire before speech is the ability to interact with people. Your baby begins to learn about this process very early on and by three months he will already be using communicative gestures. Try raising your eyebrows to him and then watch as he imitates you. This is the first stage of learning about holding a conversation. These gestures will be accompanied by different noises as your baby begins to develop control over dozens of separate muscles which are involved in making speech sounds. When your baby coos and gurgles at you he is learning to coordinate tongue movements while taking air in. When you respond to these early noises you will instinctively use a high-pitched, rhythmic singsong tone, repeating words in such a way that you capture your baby's attention.

Even a very young baby will be receptive to the sound of his mother's voice because he will have heard it in the womb.

Chat to your baby when you hold him as he will find the sound of your voice soothing and comforting.

By around five or six months, your child will be concentrating on one-syllable words such as "ba" or "ma" which he will repeat over and over again, often when he is on his own. This use of early sounds is known as babbling, and is not yet being used as a form of communication. This is your baby's way of learning how to make new sounds. Soon after he has learned to babble you will notice that your baby starts to use his eyes to communicate with you and to direct your attention towards something that he wants. This communication is soon followed by what is called declarative pointing: pointing as a form of interacting, rather than just as a basic means of asking you to pass him

If you speak to your new baby in a high-pitched, singsong voice you will immediately get his attention.

Even at the young age of eight weeks your baby will respond to your voice and attempt to smile at you.

something he can't reach for himself.

After a month or two your baby's babbling will start to flow like speech, rising and falling as if he were holding a conversation. Although he is still not able to form words, he will understand simple words which are made clear, for example, "bottle" when you point to his feeding bottle. Understanding more than he is able to say will continue throughout baby- and toddler-hood until he can speak fluently.

FIRST WORDS

By the end of his first year your baby will probably produce his first word.

It may not seem recognizable as a word to you, but it will be a sound that he uses for one specific object, for example, "ine" for when he wants an orange. It is certainly no accident that "mama" and "dada" are often among the first recogniz-able words that a new baby says, because first words are simple and are associated with things that are special to a child.

Once speech has begun with your baby, he will continue to produce a handful of new words each month with the majority of this early com-munication being simple nouns or proper names.

How you can help

• Always respond to your baby's attempts at communicating with you.

• Don't be embarrassed to use high-pitched speech; it is the language your child likes best.

• Talk to your baby as you go about your daily routine and remember to speak clearly using simple words.

• Be consistent, using the same words for the same thing every time.

• Look at simple picture books with your baby. By telling him what is in each picture you will be increasing his understanding of words.

A mother can help her child learn to talk properly by repeating words and by pointing out objects and saying the word.

TALKING

As your baby investigates colourful items, such as a yellow flower, you can talk to him about it, telling him which are the petals, leaves and stem.

SOCIAL BEHAVIOUR

A newborn baby doesn't appear very sociable to the outside world because she doesn't smile or respond verbally until some weeks after birth. But her parents' reactions to the baby's ordinary behaviour lead to the development of social mannerisms. For example, wind may cause your baby to appear to smile at an early age and you respond by smiling back. Your baby will eventually realize that this movement of her mouth makes you react in this way and so will use it deliberately in the future. It is this early, simple form of communication that is the basis for your child's social development.

All babies' early social learning comes from imitating the people with whom they have the most contact, generally their mother and father. A newborn of only a few hours can imitate some adult gestures such as poking her tongue out or yawning. This ability to imitate is one of the most important tools your baby has to help her learn about life.

Through imitation your baby will eventually start communicating. You will speak to her and she will respond with "coos" and will wriggle her body in delight. This first stage of conversation will eventually develop into the ability to talk and listen. These early conversations often start during feeding, because the rhythm of feeding initiates your baby into the basics of dialogue. A baby sucks in her mother's milk in bursts with pauses in between. It is during these pauses that her mother usually fills in the gap by talking happily to her.

IMITATION BECOMES CHOICE
Social interaction between you and your baby becomes increasingly intentional on her part during the first two months of life, with much of your baby's behaviour geared towards making you react. These early conversations and the ability to imitate are just two ways of getting you to respond; the other very effective way is crying. Initially, your baby's cries are a reflex to pain, hunger, or discomfort. But crying assures a baby of adult response, especially her mother's. Her cries will increase her mother's heart rate and, if breast-feeding, her mother will automatically start producing milk. Within a few weeks a baby will have learned to expect certain reactions to her crying, such as being fed or picked up.

At around six weeks your baby will learn to smile properly, another social skill which she will be able to use to her advantage. Although her

When young babies are placed together, they don't play with each other as they haven't yet learned how to interact. Instead they will just play on their own.

If you put two or three babies together in a playpen they will not play together as they haven't learned how to socialize.

first smiles are simply facial grimaces, your response will be such that she soon discovers that by using her facial muscles in this way she is guaranteed to get you to smile back. A baby will quickly learn to repeat an action if she gets a positive reaction. However, if she regards the response she receives as negative she is less likely to repeat the action.

By three months your baby will be able to show her enjoyment of people and surroundings. She will respond to friendly adults and will generally not mind who is with her as long as they are paying attention to her. Your baby will enjoy activities such as having a bath and often show pleasure when she realizes that bathtime has arrived. Feeding will be a great source of emotional pleasure and your baby will study your face unblinkingly while she feeds.

At around four months your baby will cry more deliberately. She will probably pause after crying to see if anyone is coming in response, before crying again. She has learned that crying brings attention and this new ability to manipulate is the beginning of some exciting discoveries.

CHANGING BEHAVIOUR PATTERNS
Somewhere after six months your child may change from a social, happy baby, who will go to anyone and reward complete strangers with smiles, to one who overnight has become wary of people she doesn't know. Your baby has reached the stage when she needs time and space to handle each new sight and sound; and a stranger may present her with too many new, unfamiliar things to be taken in at one time. This new wariness leads to what is known as stranger anxiety. It often manifests itself as loud protestations when your baby is about to be separated from you. She is at the stage of develop-

As your baby will feel safe with you, try to show her different toys and items to interest her and attract her attention.

ment when she is becoming increasingly sensitive to change and appears to be suddenly more dependent. She may try to avoid upsetting or stressful events by crying, clinging to you, or turning away from what is upsetting her. Towards the end of her first year she may start to use objects such as a favourite blanket, bottle, or thumb as a comforter.

Over the next six months your baby will probably show an increasing reticence with strangers but will be very responsive to people with whom she is familiar. She may become very clinging so that any separation from you is accompanied by real distress. This attachment may cause you problems, but it is in fact an important stage of development. Your baby now recognizes individuals as people and is beginning to develop selective, permanent relationships. She will use these relationships as a safe base from which to explore the world. Now that she is getting older, your baby will use her

A baby will sit with her brother because he is familiar. She will be interested in his toys but won't play with him.

developing vocal skills to create noise – this guarantees the attention that gives her the reassurance she needs. She may use mimicry to make you laugh and the more you show your appreciation the more she will repeat the antic which is amusing you. This is her first real control over her social environment.

By the time she is a year old, your child will probably have grasped the idea that she exists as an entity. She may even begin to use a word or

Your baby will sit quite happily on your knee, but may be wary of moving to his grandmother who is less familiar to him.

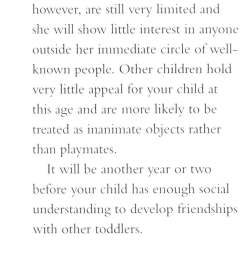

A baby will soon learn to recognize his older sister and will happily let her help him to stand up.

sound to describe herself as a means of expressing this. Her social skills, however, are still very limited and she will show little interest in anyone outside her immediate circle of well-known people. Other children hold very little appeal for your child at this age and are more likely to be treated as inanimate objects rather than playmates.

It will be another year or two before your child has enough social understanding to develop friendships with other toddlers.

How you can help

• Encourage your baby to imitate you by exaggerating your responses to her actions.

• Smile at your baby to let her know how pleased you are when she smiles at you.

• If she becomes wary of strangers don't force her to be sociable.

• When you have to leave your baby, say goodbye quickly; don't prolong the parting.

MOBILITY

All babies go through the same stages of mobility, but how fast they move from one to another varies considerably. Your baby may walk independently before he is a year old, or he may be content to shuffle along on his bottom or hands and knees until well after this. Your baby's mobility takes place in a set order, starting at his head and working down to his toes. He won't be able to sit upright or crawl until he can hold up his head, and he won't be able to walk until he can move his body along, either by crawling or doing a bottom shuffle.

Finally, your baby will learn to control his arms and legs before gaining control of his hands and feet. At each stage it will take time for the movements he has learned to progress from being awkward, rather clumsy and uncoordinated to the smooth, controlled movements he will ultimately achieve.

MAKING PROGRESS

A newborn baby has no control over his head, which will flop around if left unsupported. By about eight weeks, control of the head and neck begins and you may notice your baby practising lifting his head and holding it for a few seconds before letting it flop down again. At around three months most babies are able to hold their heads up steadily so that they can look around and examine the world about them.

The next stage in mobility comes when your baby starts to roll around, first from side to back and then, a few weeks later, from back to side. The way a baby rolls is highly individual and your baby will roll when he's ready and in his own way. Rolling is another way of practising control over his body and your baby will do it over and over again until he's mastered what to him is a new movement. The result of this

How you can help

• Hold your baby upright so he can bounce his legs up and down on your lap to help strengthen his muscles.
• Sitting a little way away from your baby, persuade him to come to you. Do this to encourage both crawling and walking.
• Once he can sit upright, you can help your baby learn to balance by placing toys slightly out of reach so he has to stretch out for them.
• To get your baby to twist around, place a toy behind him and then support him as he turns.
• Push-along toys will encourage your baby to crawl and walk.

movement will change your baby's view of the world and once he has discovered this, rolling becomes a new function: a means of getting closer to something that he wants. Your baby will have been using his legs to push with since he was born, although the first stepping movements he made as a newborn were a

All babies' first movements will be uncoordinated, but they soon learn a basic crawl and to sit upright unaided.

When your baby is placed on his stomach at a few months old he will attempt to crawl.

He will lift up his arms and legs in the swimming motion that is the prelude to crawling.

Before she's a year old, your baby will start to stand and balance holding onto a chair if you hold it steady for her.

She will grasp firmly onto the bottom part of the chair and start to pull herself up. Try to encourage her as much as possible.

As she straightens into an upright position, she will need support from the chair you are holding.

Now she is standing confidently, she will start to look around her to see what else is going on in the room.

As your baby starts to crawl, he will move towards interesting toys.

When he is nearer the toys, he will probably reach out for them.

reflex action. At around four months if you put your baby down on his abdomen, he will be able to lift his shoulders, arms, and legs off the floor and move them in a swimming-type motion, and by around five-and-a-half months your baby should be able to sit with some support, his back straight and shoulders braced. By around six months he will probably be able to support himself in a crawling position, although he won't be able to go anywhere just yet. By seven months he will be able to sit upright using his arms for support. Once he has done this he will quickly learn to sit unaided, and he will also enjoy standing and bouncing vigorously while you hold him.

By eight or nine months he will have learned to control his movements and he will be able to move his arms and legs in order to propel

himself either backwards or forwards. Once he has mastered this he will be off and it will only be a matter of time before he starts trying to stand up on his own. By about nine months he will be able to sit and reach in front, upwards, to the side and behind him without falling over.

As soon as he has learned to crawl at around nine months he will be ready to start pulling himself up into a standing position using you, or the furniture, for support. At this stage he will not have mastered sitting down so when he wants to sit he will simply let go and land down on the floor with a resounding bump. He probably won't be able to control his sitting movement until he is 11 to 12 months old.

Before he's a year old your baby

will start to navigate all around the furniture, taking little sideways steps. Once he can move around like this with some confidence he will let go with one hand. As soon as he is able to let go with his remaining hand, perhaps to cross a gap in the furniture, he will begin to get the confidence to walk about unaided.

Your baby's first steps on his own will be very wobbly and ungainly, with his feet placed wide apart to help him balance. But once he becomes more mobile his legs will straighten and he'll become steadier on his feet.

By eight or nine months your baby will be able to crawl around on the floor.

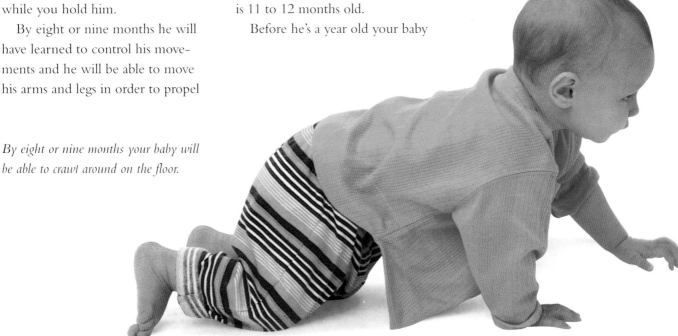

Your baby will try to stand with your help.

Lift him up supporting his arms.

Once up, he will need your hand to balance.

A baby walker can help a child to take her first steps and practise walking.

Once crawling your baby will go all over.

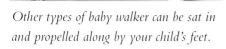

Other types of baby walker can be sat in and propelled along by your child's feet.

A young baby will enjoy a baby bouncer, but make sure it is firmly attached.

Your child's first steps are often wobbly and his movements may seem awkward.

PLAY

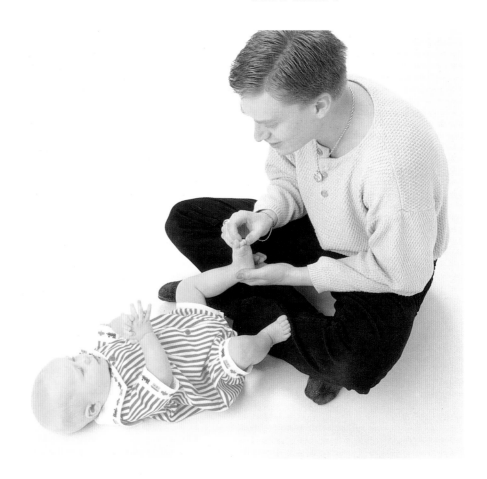

Introduce your baby to games by teaching him nursery rhymes like "this little piggy went to market".

A baby is born with the potential to learn and play. She can see, hear, and feel. She is aware of her environment and will respond from birth to brightly coloured, moving objects and to sounds. She learns all the time and play is one of the ways in which she develops new skills, while toys are the play tools that she uses to stimulate herself at each stage of development. Toys don't have to be elaborate; your child will invent her own games and use everyday objects as toys when she is young. Watching you and trying to imitate your voice and facial expressions will provide hours of entertainment in the early months. Ultimately, the toy that a child enjoys and plays with most will give her the greatest learning experience, and in the first weeks of life this "toy" will be you.

Your child will change very rapidly during the first year so that a toy that entertains her at two months will not appeal to her when she is a year old. As she develops, your child will need different stimuli and the choice of toys for each stage of development should reflect these different needs. It is also very important that the toys you give a child are appropriate to this age. A toy designed for a younger child will be boring, while a toy for an older child may be too complicated and may even be dangerous if it contains small pieces on which a young baby could choke.

BIRTH TO THREE MONTHS

During the first few months, your baby is developing her basic senses – touch, sight, and sound. She needs

Your child will be fascinated by nursery rhymes that involve actions that use his hands.

Because the end of "round and round the garden" includes tickling your baby, he will associate it with fun and ask for more.

As your child develops she will start to enjoy playing games with you such as "peek-a-boo".

As you teach her the game, she will enjoy "hiding" behind the chair and peeking out at you from behind the legs.

Games to play

• Gently bounce your baby up and down on your knee in rhythm to a nursery rhyme.

• Hold her palm open and play "round and round the garden" ending up with a tickle under her arm.

• Use her toes to play "this little piggy went to market".

• Take your baby as your partner and dance around the room with her in your arms.

You can buy your baby many expensive toys, but she'll still enjoy playing with simple kitchen utensils. Always make sure they have no sharp edges.

toys which will stimulate these senses and give experience of colours, textures, materials, and shapes. A good first toy is a mobile, hung where your baby can study it at leisure. It doesn't have to be expensive – one made from pictures cut from a magazine and suspended from a coat hanger will be just as effective as one you buy. Once your baby begins to wave her hands around and tries to swipe at things, she will enjoy toys that make a noise or that react to her actions, a rattle for example. This will give your child a sense of control as well as encouraging the development of manual skills and hand and eye co-ordination.

A newborn baby's hands are usually held closed in fists, but she will gradually relax them so that if you place an object in her open palm she will close her hand around it for a few seconds. The strong grasp reflex she was born with will have disappeared so that she will probably drop the object within a few seconds. By the

An activity centre is ideal for babies around nine months as they will love to push the buttons and manipulate all the different shapes and knobs.

age of two or three months she will try reaching out to touch things. These first grasping movements are important steps towards learning hand-eye co-ordination.

Once your baby is old enough to sit in a bouncing cradle she will be able to see more of the world around her and her hands will be free to explore. A toy fastened across the front of the cradle will encourage her to bring her hands forward to try and hit it to make it move. Once she has done this, she will want to do it again and again; gradually she sees that she is responsible for making this happen and her movements become more deliberate.

A newborn is acutely aware of sounds and will already have become familiar with your voice while in the womb. Talking and singing to your baby from the time she is born will encourage her to listen and help her develop her own speech later. As she gets older, hold her on your lap and try having a conversation with her. Say something, then wait until your baby makes a noise in response. Her response will be slow at first so allow her plenty of time. These conversations will help her learn about taking turns, listening, and copying – all essential parts of communication. Once your baby has got used to life

As she starts to move around, your baby will get pleasure from pushing a baby walker. She will also enjoy trying to put plastic shapes in the right holes on the walker.

outside the womb, she will find touch and the freedom to move her limbs exciting. Different textures will give her new sensations of touch, so offer her various things to feel that will give her experience of rough, soft, silky, or smooth textures. Bathing and changing times will provide an opportunity for your baby to explore touch and sensation. She will like the feeling of not being hampered by nappies and clothing and should enjoy the sensation of warm water next to her skin. Try tickling her gently, blowing raspberries on her abdomen, and kissing her toes when she is undressed.

THREE TO SIX MONTHS

As your baby grows and her movements become more controlled, she will reach out for things and take them in her hands. Her grip becomes stronger and she will be able to hold a wider variety of items. This means that she will start to experience the difference between things that are light and heavy, soft and hard. Her curiosity will be endless and every object will be a plaything. She may prefer to use her mouth rather than her hands to explore things at this age, so it is important to make sure that she can't get hold of anything which could do her any harm.

Your baby will probably play happily for short periods on her own, but she needs you to encourage her. When you play with your baby get her to do things for herself; allow her to use her hands and eyes to work out what she wants to do with the toy she is holding. It is better to give your child only a few selected items to play with at this age because she won't be able to concentrate on more than one thing at a time. A

stimulating, inviting environment is important for all creative play. Toys that are piled up in a jumble are not as inviting to a child as toys which are laid out for her in an attractive, inviting way.

SIX TO TWELVE MONTHS

Once your baby has learned to support herself sitting up and has started to make her first attempts at moving around, she will want toys that she can manipulate. This is the ideal time to give your child an activity centre with lots of different knobs and handles for her to twist and turn. By around seven or eight

months she will want to find out what things can do and will bang objects on the ground or table to find out if they make a noise or wave them in the air to see what happens. As her manipulative skills develop she will learn that she can use her hands and arms simultaneously and will start to bang things together. She will be able to reach out to you with both arms when she wants to be picked up. It takes a while longer for her to learn how to let go of items she is playing with, but you can encourage her by giving her an object, then holding out your hand and asking for it back. Once she's

A young baby will enjoy being read to from a simple board book and will be interested in touching the pages. She will soon learn how to recognize the book's pictures.

can put things back into the container and will spend ages tipping things out and putting them back again. She will try doing this with different objects and may discover that some of them don't fit. As your child plays she will be learning about the nature of the objects, how they behave, and their relative size and shape.

Water play can be introduced now and your baby will enjoy filling and emptying plastic beakers while she is having her bath. Give her toys which have different sizes of holes in them so that she can spend time sprinkling or pouring the water from one container into another.

Once your baby has started to crawl, give her toys that roll and move when they are pushed along so that she can go after them. Later, as she starts taking her weight on her legs, you can encourage her and help her balance with sturdy push-along toys, such as a brick trolley. This will

Your child will often put different things in her mouth to investigate them.

got the hang of this game she will keep you busy for hours!

As she becomes more mobile, your baby will want to be into everything and her natural curiosity could lead her into danger, so you need to pay constant attention to safety. One of your baby's favourite pastimes will be emptying things out of containers. She will take things out of cupboards with just as much enjoyment as she will empty shapes out of a shape sorter. Once she has emptied a container she will want to examine the contents in great detail and will bang things together and may put them in her mouth before discarding them and moving on to the next object. When she has mastered this she will soon learn that she

A baby walker will help your child to walk and some double as an activity centre.

give her something to hold onto until she feels confident enough to let go and walk unaided.

BOOKS

It is never too early to introduce your baby to books. Start at an early age with brightly coloured rag books that your baby can chew as well as handle, or simple board books. At first she will enjoy these books as objects to be explored but, if you sit her on your knee and talk to her about the pictures in the book, she will soon learn to recognize them. Encourage her involvement by making the noises of any animals pictured in the books and then getting her to do the same.

Games to play

• "Pat-a-cake, pat-a-cake, baker's man" is a rhyme to which your baby will enjoy clapping. When you get to "prick it and pat it and mark it with ..." use your baby's own initial and then her name when you come to "put in the oven for ...".

• Blowing bubbles using either a made-up solution and a wand or washing-up liquid and your hands.

• "Peek-a-boo": use your hands to cover your face; then later hide and seek: hide objects under a soft cloth for your baby to find.

• Hold your baby's hands securely and rock her gently backwards and forward while singing "Row, row, row the boat ...".

• Sit your baby on your knee facing towards you and hold her firmly by the hands as you bounce her in time to "Humpty Dumpty". When you get to the big fall allow your baby to drop through your knees while holding her firmly.

By just giving your baby one toy at a time to play with, she will be able to concentrate on it more fully.

Your young baby will enjoy looking at a toy hung from the pram or above the cot.

Toys for 0-6 months
- Mobile.
- Rattle.
- Soft toys.
- Baby mirror.
- Squeaker.
- Baby gym.
- Play mat.

Toys for 7-12 months
- Cloth or card books.
- Big ball.
- Soft blocks.
- Beakers.
- Bath toys.
- Pop-up toys.
- Musical toys.
- Push-along toys.

This rollaball can be rolled along and will help your baby's hand/eye co-ordination.

Simple toys which are colourful, tactile and chewable will interest a young baby.

As your baby learns to co-ordinate his hands, he will like to hold and feel toys that are easy to handle. This frog also has a baby-safe mirror. Your baby will be fascinated by his own reflection.

A play telephone with push buttons that make different noises will intrigue your baby and keep him amused for hours.

This colourful activity octopus has eight different-textured tentacles for your young baby to grasp and pull at. The caterpillar can be bent into different positions.

Your older baby will enjoy playing with different-sized, coloured stacking beakers.

This stacker has different coloured rings to help an older baby recognize colours and learn how to stack the rings.

This shape sorter offers your child the opportunity to explore different shapes as well as colours.

Once your baby can sit unaided he will enjoy toys such as this train that he can push along the floor.

A simple shape sorter will give your older baby hours of entertainment as he discovers how to put the squares into the holes and then watch them drop inside.

All babies enjoy an activity centre and one that can be fixed to the side of the cot will keep your baby amused when you put him down for a rest.

Pull-along toys will develop and encourage your baby's mobility. They will also help him gain confidence as he learns how to push and pull the toy back and forth along the length of the floor.

USEFUL ADDRESSES

There is no need to feel alone in the months after the birth.
The organizations mentioned below are happy to offer help and support to anyone who contacts them.
Remember to enclose an SAE when writing to them.

ANTE-NATAL AND BIRTH
Active Birth Centre, Bickerton House, 25 Bickerton Road, London N19 5JT. Tel: 0171-561 9006

Association for Improvements in the Maternity Services (AIMS), 40 Kingswood Avenue, London NW6 6LS. Tel: 0181-960 5585

Association of Radical Midwives (ARM), 62 Greetby Hill, Ormskirk, Lancs. L39 2DT. Tel: 01695-572776

BLISS (Information for parents of special-care babies), 17-21 Emerald Street, London WC1N 3QL. Tel: 0171-831 9393

British Pregnancy Advisory Service (BPAS), Austy Manor, Wootton Wawen, Solihull, West Midlands B95 6BX. Helpline: 01564-793225

Foresight (The Association for the Promotion of Conceptual Care), 28 The Paddock, Godalming, Surrey GU7 1XD. Tel/fax: 01483-427839. Contact at least four months prior to planned conception.

Foundation for the Study of Infant Deaths (Cot Death Research & Support), 14 Halkin Street, London SW1X 7DP. Tel: 0171-235 0965 24-hour helpline: 0171-235 1721

Independent Midwives Association, Nightingale Cottage, Shamblehurst Lane, Botley, Hants. SO32 2BY. (No phone number, but please send A5 SAE for register of independent midwives)

Maternity Alliance, 15 Britannia Street, London WC1X 9JN.

Tel: 0171-837 1265 (Mon, Tues, Thurs, Fri 9am–1pm. Wed 2pm–5pm)

The Miscarriage Association, c/o Clayton Hospital, Northgate, Wakefield, W. Yorks. WF1 3JS. Tel: 01924 200799 (answerphone out of office hours)

National Childbirth Trust (NCT), Alexandra House, Oldham Terrace, London W3 6NH. Tel: 0181-992 8637

Stillbirth and Neonatal Death Society (SANDS), 28 Portland Place, London W1N 4DE. Tel: 0171-436 7940 Helpline: 0171-436 5881 (10am–5.30pm)

Toxoplasmosis Trust, 61-71 Collier Street, London N1 9BE. Helpline: 0171-713 0599

WellBeing (Health Research Charity for Women and Babies), 27 Sussex Place, Regent's Park, London NW1 4SP. Tel: 0171-262 5337

FAMILY LINKS
Gingerbread, 49 Wellington Street, London WC2E 7BN. Tel: 0171-240 0953

Meet a Mum Association, 14 Willis Road, Croydon, Surrey CR0 2XX. Tel: 0181-665 0357. Also post-natal depression and general advice. Helpline: 0181-656 7318.

National Childminding Association 8 Masons Hill, Bromley, Kent BR2 9EY. Tel: 0181-464 6164

National Council for One Parent Families, 255 Kentish Town Road, London NW5 2LX. Tel: 0171-267 1361

Working for Childcare, 77 Holloway Road, London N7 8JZ. Tel: 0171-700 0281

SPECIAL NEEDS
ASBAH (Association for Spina Bifida and Hydrocephalus), 42 Park Road, Peterborough PE1 2UQ. Tel: 01733 555988

British Diabetic Association, 10 Queen Anne Street, London W1M 0BD. Tel: 0171-323 1531

British Epilepsy Association, Anstey House, 40 Hanover Square, Leeds LS3 1BE. Free helpline: 0800 309030

Cystic Fibrosis Trust, Alexandra House, 5 Blyth Road, Bromley, Kent BR1 3RS. Tel: 0181-464 7211

Down's Syndrome Association, 155 Mitcham Road, London SW17 9PG. Tel: 0181-682 4001

Galactosaemia Support Group, 31 Cotysmore Road, Sutton Coldfield B75 6BJ. Tel: 0121-378 5143

Mencap (Royal Society for Mentally Handicapped Children and Adults), 123 Golden Lane, London EC1Y 0RT. Tel: 0171-454 0454

National Asthma Campaign,
Providence House, Providence Place,
London N1 0NT.
Tel: 0171-226 2260
Helpline: 0345 010203
(Mon to Fri 9am–9pm)

National Autistic Society,
276 Willesden Lane, London
NW2 5RB. Tel: 0181-451 1114

National Deaf Children's Society,
15 Dufferin Street, London EC1Y 8PD.
Tel: 0171-250 0123

National Eczema Society,
163 Eversholt Street, London
NW1 1BU.
Tel: 0171-388 4097

**Research Trust for Metabolic
Diseases in Children (RTMDC),**
Golden Gates Lodge, Weston Road,
Crewe CW1 1XN.
Tel: 01270 250221

**Royal National Institute for the
Blind (RNIB),** 224 Great Portland
Street, London W1N 6AA.
Tel: 0171-388 1266

Scope (formerly Spastics Society), 12
Park Crescent, London W1N 4EQ.
Tel: 0171-636 5020

SENSE (National Deaf-Blind and Rubella
Association), 11-13 Clifton Terrace,
Finsbury Park, London N4 3SR.
Tel: 0171-272 7774

Sickle Cell Society, 54 Station Road,
Harlesden, London NW10 4UA.
Tel: 0181-961 7795 (Mon to Fri
9am–5pm)

**Voluntary Council for Handicapped
Children,** 8 Wakley Street, London
EC1V 7QE.
Tel: 0171-843 6000

FOR NEW PARENTS
**Association of Breastfeeding
Mothers,** 26 Holmshaw Close, London

SE26 4TH.
Tel: 0181-778 4769

Association for Post-Natal Illness,
25 Jerdan Place, London SW6 1BE.
Tel: 0171-386 0868
(answerphone out of office hours)

Cry-sis, BM Cry-sis, London WC1N
3XX (Counsellors available between
9am–11pm)
Tel: 0171-404 5011

La Leche League of Great Britain,
PO Box BM 3424, London WC1N
3XX.
Tel: 0171-242 1278. Helps and supports
women who wish to breast-feed. (24-
hour counselling service)

FAMILY WELFARE
Action for Sick Children, Argyle
House, 29-31 Euston Road,
London NW1 2SD.
Tel: 0171-833 2041 (Mon to Fri
9am–5pm)

Children's Legal Centre,
The University of Essex, Wivenhoe
Park, Colchester, Essex CO4 3SQ.
Tel: 01206 873820

Citizen's Advice Bureau,
address and telephone number for
your nearest office in your local telephone book.

Compassionate Friends, 53 North
Street, Bristol BS3 1EN.
Helpline: 0117 953 9639 (Mon to Fri
9.30am - 5pm)

Contact-a-Family, 170 Tottenham
Court Road, London W1P OHA.
Tel: 0171-383 3555

Cruse (Bereavement Care),
Cruse House, 126 Sheen Road,
Richmond, Surrey TW9 1UR.
Bereavement line: 0181-332 7227
(Mon to Fri 9.30am–5pm)

Family Planning Association, 27-35
Mortimer Street, London W1N 7RJ.
Tel: 0171-636 7866

Family Welfare Association,
501-505 Kingsland Road, London
E8 4AU.
Tel: 0171-254 6251

**National Association for the Welfare
of Children in Hospital (NAWCH),**
Argyle House, 29-31 Euston Road,
London NW1 2SD.
Tel: 0171-833 2041

**National Childcare
Campaign/Daycare Trust,** 4 Wild
Court, London WC2B 4AU.
Tel: 0171-405 5617

**National Society for the Prevention
of Cruelty to Children (NSPCC),**
National Centre, 42 Curtain Road,
London EC2A 3NH.
Tel: 0800 800 500
(free 24-hour confidential helpline)

Relate (National Marriage Guidance),
Herbert Gray College, Little Church
Street, Rugby, Warks CV21 3AP, or
look in telephone directory under "R"
for Relate or "M" for Marriage Guidance.

SAFTA (Support after termination for
abnormality), 73-75 Charlotte Street,
London W1P 1LB.
Tel: 0171-631 0285

Samaritans,
Tel: 0345 909090 (24-hour confidential
helpline). For local number look in your
telephone directory.

Smokers' Quitline,
Tel: 0171-487 3000

**Twins and Multiple Births
Association (TAMBA),** PO Box 30,
Little Sutton, South Wirral L66 1TH.
Tel: 0151-348 0020 (Mon to Fri
9am–1pm)

Vegetarian Society,
Parkdale, Dunham Road, Altrincham,
Cheshire WA14 4QG.
Tel: 0161 9280793

INDEX

ACKNOWLEDGEMENTS

The author and publisher would like to thank the many individuals who helped in the creation of this book.
In particular thanks are due to Bobbie Brown, Elsa Jacobi, Pauline Richardson, Mary Lambert and Jane Barret.
Many thanks also go to everyone who modelled for special photography: Yvonne Adams and Martin; Ruth Auber and Bethany;
Jo Bates and Lois; Amanda Bennet-Jones; Kim, Neil and Andrew Brown; Christine Clarke; Jacqueline Clarke and Cassia;
Jocelyn Cusack and Beth; Sam Dyas and Colt; Patricia Gannon and Matthew; Nici Giles and Fergus; Yiota Gillis and Cameron;
Sandra Hadfield and Annie; Louise Henriques and Joshua; Lynette Jones and Hugh and Rhys; Karen, Mark, Megan and
Robert Lambert; Claire Lehain and Harriet; Lavinia Mainds and Polly; Pippa Milton and Oliver; Philippa Madden and Inca;
Jackie Norbury; Jess Presland; Katey Steiner; Saatchi Spracklen and Niamh; Sophie Trotter and Archie;
Josephine Whitfield and Lily May; Lucinda Whitrow and Hector.
Thanks also to companies who loaned items and photographs:
Boots Children's Wear and Toys, Fisher-Price, Littlewoods Home Shopping, Maclaren Ltd and Mattel UK Ltd.

PICTURE ACKNOWLEDGEMENTS
Bubbles /Jacquie Farrow 51; /S.Price 22 bottom; /Loisjoy Thurston 12, 22 top, 42, 43; /
Ian West 47 bottom right; /**Lupe Cunha** 10 right; **Science Photo Library** /Mark Clarke 19; /Simon Fraser 19 bottom.
The publishers have tried to credit all agencies and photographers whose pictures appear
in this book and apologize for any omissions.